Eco Media

Contemporary Cinema 1

Contemporary Cinema is a series of edited volumes and single-authored texts focusing on the latest in film culture, theory, reception and interpretation. There is a concentration on films released in the past fifteen years, and the aim is to reflect important current issues while pointing to others that to date have not been given sufficient attention.

Eco Media

Sean Cubitt

Rodopi

Amsterdam - New York, NY 2005

Institutional support:
The Department of Theatre, Film and Television Studies at the University of Wales-Aberystwyth

The paper on which this book is printed meets the requirements of "ISO 9706:1994, Information and documentation - Paper for documents - Requirements for permanence".

ISBN: 90-420-1885-2
ISSN: 1572-3070

Printed in the Netherlands

For Paddy and the Parnabys

Contents

One of the jobs intellectuals do is making new arguments. The greatest breakthroughs, Kuhn's paradigm shifts, are the moments of greatest novelty. So much professional kudos accrues to these innovations that they will always tempt the scholar - 'the last infirmity of noble mind'. Rather than thinking of intellectual life as grand prix of each against all, I prefer to consider it in terms of a greener sport, cycling's Tour de France. The Tour is a team event, with squads working to get their rider to the front for each of the point-scoring opportunities, a rider specialising in each of the sprints, hill-climbs, time-trials, and one they will try to position to win the overall race winner's maillot jaune. More peculiar is the structure of a typical day's racing. The majority of the riders travel in a bunch, the pelloton, using the turbulence behind the leaders to reduce the airpressure in their faces, and taking turns at the front to keep the whole pack moving. Every now and then a daring soul springs off the front to make a dash for victory, always tearing a handful of riders in pursuit, a cluster that will also work together to maintain their lead before trying to snatch the win at the final line. Meanwhile the pelloton accelerate to catch the breakaway, dragging with them the slowest riders sitting at the back. This strange combination of mutual aid and competition depends of course on a certain elitism: only the toughest riders will complete the three week race, so only the toughest enter. In a given field of intellectual endeavour, that is also the case. After all the long months of solitary practice, we media scholars set off, each taking a turn at the front in service of the rest, sometimes in small bands tearing off ahead, setting a new pace, creating the groundswell of speed that allows the best to make those suddeen leaps to glory, while very often the most successful of all will spend most of the race in the pelloton, shoulder to shoulder, taking their turn, consistent, cunning. Alas there is no final line in the tour of media. By the same token, there is no winner, except that to take part is a delight, and to stay the course a triumph, especially in the company of such a fine peloton.

When I began work on it, this book was intended as a swift exercise in the interpretation of popular films. It has become something a lot more demanding. Research on this project was supported by a study leave granted by the Faculty of Arts and Social Sciences at the University of Waikato, Hamilton; and by visiting fellowships at The Australia Centre of the University of Melbourne and the Robards Centre for Canadian Studies at York University, Toronto. My thanks for help in this project to John Armitage, Martin Barker, Andy Barrett, Neil Bather, Pat Brereton, Jane Button, Stella Brennan, Nigel Clark, Ian Conrich, Rosemary Coombe, Judith Doyle, Seth Feldman, James Gillespie, Phil Graham, John Grayson, Alistair Gunn, Andrew Herman, Aneta P, Janet Jones, Steve Jones, Ryszard Kluczinski, Elle Leane, Bill MacArthur, Ernest Matthijs, Scott McQuire, Adrian Miles, Shaun Moores, Angela Ndalianis, John Pace, Nikos Papastergiadis, Randy Rutsky, Zia Sardar, Steven Schneider, Christa Stevens, Nell Tenhaaf and my colleagues on the *Lord of the Rings* projects and especially to the Screen Team at the University of Waikato, than whom there can be no more exciting, collegial and stimulating pals. Special thanks to Janine Marchessault, Bob Hahnke and Jody Berland for inspiring dialogues; to Steven Schneider as editor on the series and to the ever courteous and efficient BFI Stills Library. As ever, all my gratitude and love to Alison with some left over for Zebedee, whose companionship also inspired this book, which is gratefully dedicated to my sister and her family for their love and support.

Part of chapter 2 was presented as a graduate seminar in Cinema Studies at the University of Melbourne in April 2004, part of chapter 6 was first given as a paper at the Screen Conference, University of Glasgow 4-6 July 2003, and part of chapter 5 at the Society for Cinema and Media Studies, Atlanta, 2004. Many of the themes of chapters 3, 4, 5 and 7 were worked through in public lectures and with graduate students at York University, Toronto, in May 2004, whose company, good spirits and readiness to disagree made workng on the book harder but much more fun.

1 Introduction

> Mankind, which in Homer's time was an object of contemplation for the Olympian gods, now is one for itself. Its self-alienation has reached such a degree that it can experience its own destruction as an aesthetic pleasure of the first order. (Benjamin 1969: 242)

This book is about environmental themes in popular media since the 1980s. It wants to make a contribution to ecological politics by studying popular mediations of frequently voiced concerns over biosecurity, anthropomorphism, environmental ethics, over-exploitation of resources, ecoterrorism, genetic modification and global climate change. It scrutinises some films and television programmes in order to see what they are made of, how they handle their materials, and what they say. Green parties, scientists, corporations and public intellectuals have many professional institutions that speak about the relationship between humans and nature. But they rarely have reason to speak about, let alone on behalf of, the everyday appreciation of ecological themes. Film and television creatives, on the other hand, whether they work in the pubic service tradition or from commercial imperatives, have good reason to try to hear and respond to ordinary beliefs, anxieties and ethical dilemmas about life on earth. In the absence of citizens' media, we have no better place to look than the popular media for representations of popular knowledge and the long-term concerns so little addressed in dominant political and economic discourse. In their own way as complex as the language of scientific papers or policy documents, popular media think aloud and in public about who we are, where we are going, and what debts we owe to the world we live in.

Like Pat Brereton, to whose *Hollywood Utopias* I am indebted, I am fascinated by the utopian content of popular media. But I am also fascinated by what that utopianism can tell me about the weaknesses of ecological thought and environmental politics. Though many films are predictably bound to the common ideologies of the day, including ideologies of nature, many are far richer in contradictions and more ethically, emotionally and intellectually satisfying than much of what passes for eco-politics today. Fine art and popular media alike can, at their best, be far more than symptoms of their age. They can voice its contradictions in ways few more self-conscious activities do, because both want to appeal directly to the senses, the emotions and the tastes of the hour, because both will sacrifice linear reason for rhetoric or affect, and because both have the option of abandoning the given world in favour of the image of something other than what, otherwise, we might feel we had no choice but to inhabit.

Where I part company with Brereton is in his commitment to 'the utopian spatial aesthetic that permeates Hollywood film'. While the postmodern turn to space is indeed fundamental for ecological criticism, the loss of the temporal, and especially of historical process, from ecological thought would be disastrous. The analyses of *EcoMedia* pursue that historical dimension. The quest has not proved as simple as it first seemed. The principle attraction of ecology for a media scholar is that it is a systems-oriented mode of practice and analysis where, as in media, the communication between the elements of a system is even more important, and precedes, the elements themselves: no individuals without the biosphere. But by the same token the model it offers is fundamentally ahistorical unless and until it is broken. The act of breakage is the moment of history. The biosphere itself has no history. In effect, that model of pristine nature is as politically responsible for the division of humans from nature as humanity's assaults on the green world. But if humans do inhabit and produce history, and if, as at least some green theorists argue, there is continuity between human and natural worlds, then the biosphere must be a history-generating system. In short, it must be capable of change.

Thomas Sebeok, the distinguished semiotician and specialist in animal communication, offers this definition: 'Whatever else an animal may be, it is clear that each is a living system, or subsystem, a complex array of atoms organized and maintained according to certain principles, the most important among these being negative entropy' (Sebeok 1991: 159). The most obvious articulation of human and natural worlds being the human animal, this definition gives us several starting points. Living creatures are made of atoms, that is, of matter and energy. These atoms are structured in arrays, that is, they have dimensionality, occupying space. Since Einstein, we know that space and time are inseparable, and in any case the concept of entropy brings with it the physics of time. We are also systems maintained in negative entropy, that is, against the flow of time announced in the second law of thermodynamics, according to which any system will tend towards a state of rest. This law is interpreted in information and cybernetic theory as indicating that systems tend to lose structure over time. Negative entropy indicates the contrary: that living systems either maintain themselves against entropy, or indeed, in processes of evolution and socialisation, may perhaps also tend towards higher states of complex organisation rather than lower ones.

The inference is that living organisms are composed of information. The physical (matter-energy) aspects of life are only lightly touched on in the current work: the reader is referred to Eugene Thacker's (2004) remarkable *Biomedia* and its analysis of biological technologies of communication for a sense of what remains to be discussed there. The dimensional (space-time) component is significant not only for linking the spatial orientation of scientific ecology with the historical orientation of the humanities, but because dimensionality, notoriously hard to define, is as much a matter of experience, perception and social construction as it is a given. With the informational aspect, in Bateson's classic aphorism 'differences that make a difference' (Bateson 1973: 351), systems theory, the heart of ecology, meets communication. These three terms provide a skeletal machine for thinking with that informs the rest of this book. Analysis is essential because both the mediasphere and the planetary ecology are simply too vast and too complex to consider at a single stroke. But analysis requires distinguishing the moments of a single process from one another. Where possible it should be borne in mind that this analysis, derived from contemporary scientific thinking and intended to ground what follows in materialism, is only imperfectly and at times metaphorically applicable to human affairs, where other models might extrapolate other moments.

One risk of the model adopted here is that it may too easily appear timeless. Understanding how history enters what otherwise seem ahistorical terms like humanity and nature is the core rationale for studying popular media. Nuances and shadings of anxiety, aspirations and love of the green world shift slowly but visibly in reaction to a vast array of changing currents. Some of the potential contradictions that emerge in such finely-tuned changes is caught in Horkheimer's analysis of the role of mimesis in Nazism. The natural mimetic impulses of children, their pleasure in imitating, has to be overcome by civilisation, in a movement from sympathetic magic to scientific knowledge, a process in which, he remarks, 'the formula supplants the image' (Horkheimer 1992: 115). In National Socialist meetings, however, the imitation of stereotypical Jewish attributes, 'ridiculing and attacking racial enemies accused of impudently flaunting their own mimetic habits . . . aroused raucous hilarity, because a forbidden natural urge was permitted to assert itself without fear of reprimand' (Horkheimer 1992: 117). 'Hitler', Horkheimer argues, 'appealed to the unconscious in his audience by hinting that he could forge a power in whose name the ban on repressed nature would be lifted' (Horkheimer 1992: 120). The superficiality of civilisation is revealed in this rebellion of nature, a rebellion against which rational argument and democratic politics are impotent, unless they sacrifice themselves as reason and democracy in some parallel appeal to their incommensurable other. Such rapid oscillations between a position and its opposite are characteristic of the dialectical analysis of media and communication, and it is a quiet ambition of this book to suggest that a marriage of systems theory and dialectics is the most potent option available for advancing understanding of the political and social aspects of mediation, not least those pertaining to ecological themes and practices.

Anyone who picks up this book will probably already be convinced of the value of changing our exploitative relation with nature. I have not, therefore, tried to convince the reader of the need to be concerned. Instead I have tried to develop arguments expressed in popular mediations that query some of the more or less consciously held tenets of ecopolitics. A key argument is that not all technologies are instrumental, that is, used as instruments for domination over nature or other humans. Instead the book argues that both scientific and entertainment media rely on technologies to communicate between human and natural worlds. In an effort to shake existing presuppositions about the relationship, my own as much as the reader's, the word *techne* is used frequently in the book to designate not just machinery but such techniques as language and gesture that mediate between the green world and the human. Likewise the word *physis* denotes the green world, in order to emphasise both the involvement of the whole of nature, from solar radiation to soil bacteria and the processual nature of the physical universe. And finally the term *polis* is used in place of both human and society, in order both to assert the fundamentally social shape of human life and to permit the suggestion that the boundaries between the three domains may not be so robust, nor the oppositions between them so entrenched, as must often seem the case. The old Greek words are uncomfortable in 21st century English, but the wealth of their histories and their very unfamiliarity make it easier to cast off habits of thought and to reach for new ways of thinking.

Though I was delighted to be able to undertake research in Canada and Australia, I have drawn my inspiration from my new home in Aotearoa New Zealand. Here many of the generalisations of Northern sociologists and media theorists do not hold good: animals are not unfamiliar; death is not so hidden; the wilderness of the ocean is rarely more than forty miles away, and distance and a small population have preserved far more of the natural environment and the rural way of life than is common elsewhere. At the same time, the country sits for half the year under the ozone hole, with skin cancer a constant threat; the climate is changing noticeably; urban expansion and highway construction and all the ailments of larger industrial economies are here too. This is why the first chapter begins with *The Lord of the Rings* trilogy, and the issue of biosecurity, of great importance to New Zealand and Australia, though perhaps less obvious elsewhere: parallels exist with SARS in Canada, rabies in the United Kingdom, BSE and foot and mouth disease throughout the world. But the common conception of the natural habitat as something in need of protection is the real object of the chapter.

Chapter Three turns to animation, enquiring into the passion for drawing and animating animals, with the example of the anime *Mononoke Hime* (*Princess Mononoke*). Unlike some other recent animations like *Chicken Run* and *Finding Nemo*, both of which also address ecological themes, *Mononoke* also speaks to ancient beliefs in communication with animal gods, a theme close to both the more mystical trends in ecosophical thought and to the resuscitation of interest in first peoples' wisdom about how to live well in a particular bioregion. Chapter Four looks at the popular communication of science and the BBC's *The Blue Planet*, trying to tease out theses about environmental ethics from a series which never directly addresses the despoliation of the oceans, but instead devotes itself to wonder at them. *The Perfect Storm* portrays a complex meteorological event that intertwines with the economics of over-fishing, focusing on a heroic struggle for survival. The theme of the hero is as dear to eco-warrior hearts as to any audience, yet the cost of the heroic has also to be analysed. It is contrasted in Chapter Five with *Whale Rider*, a film which offers a very different conception of time and history, and therefore a different notion of heroism. Another BBC series, this time a drama, *Edge of Darkness*, forms the focus of Chapter Six. Public service broadcasting gives political drama a powerful platform, but one that for that reason is ripe with contradictions. Heroism of yet another kind comes into play here, and the issue of the status of the human in environmental politics raises its head. The theme is carried on in Chapter Seven, which looks at the Marvel franchise, and especially at the *X-men* movies as showcases for debates over the meaning and morality of genetic modification. Here the critical issue arises of the grounds on which ethical decisions can be made, and the case argued that in the early 21st century, ethics may have to give way to politics as a proper mode of debate. And politics then forms the substantial core of Chapter Eight, where *The Day After Tomorrow* provokes a discussion of the difference between a heroic ethics of antagonism and a dialectical and dialogic politics of negotiation. The conclusions brings these themes together to argue for the centrality of mediation as a core concept for understanding the ways in which the physical, technological and political worlds evolve inextricably together.

In what follows I have kept to what I know: the Western tradition. I have addressed the reader as 'we' for stylistic reasons, but also frankly as an English-speaking person with an ecological interest and a grounding in the humanities and social science traditions of media scholarship. I do not believe this is the only way to speak of these matters, but it is the only way that I am equipped to speak about in public. There is so much interest in the intersections of media and ecology at present that it is unlikely we will have to wait long for an author to address the lacunae of this work, which follows earlier pioneers like David Ingram (2000) and Jhan Hochman (1998) at the beginnings of a new enquiry.

Mediating Middle Earth:

Talking to Trees in Peter Jackson's *The Lord of the Rings*

Nature enter me
(Fourmyula, 'Nature')

Aotearoa
In 2001 a poll seeking Aotearoa New Zealand's most popular song came out overwhelmingly in favour of Fourmyula's light, frothy pop tune 'Nature'. Nostalgia, a self-image of clean, green, rural, open-air culture, pride in a relatively early home-grown hit, and the sheer pleasure of familiarity no doubt played their part. The folksy acoustic guitars and distant evocation of church choir harmonies in the chorus underpin the song's anthemic call, and indicate a prescient alertness on the part of the songwriter to the significance of environmentalism in the politics of Aotearoa particular potency in a country whose adoption of a nuclear-free policy marked it internationally as a country with a distinctive commitment to the environment. The bombing of the Rainbow Warrior in Auckland harbour – and the subsequent sinking of the wreck to provide an artificial reef – kept that commitment in the world's eye. For those of us who live here, Aotearoa's unique ecology is a source of pride and commitment, qualities which Peter Jackson's trilogy *The Lord of the Rings* reiterates in important ways for local audiences. Equally significant, however, are the rearticulations of a less parochial ecological aesthetic on behalf of the global audience which a project with this scale of budget must address. Site of all the locations and home to most of the miniature and computer generated image (CGI) material in the film, Aotearoa New Zealand's place in recent eco-political history has been reafffirmed by images of its landscapes unfolding on screens across the world. The country has not become Middle Earth, as some of the tourist board campaigns suggest, but it has achieved a certain imaginary power, as a utopian landscape for fantasies of a different humanity in tune with its world. The country evoked in the films is an environmental paradise kept free by sundering seas of the industrial and genetic pollution of the Northern hemisphere.

Aotearoa New Zealand: the double naming of the country juxtaposes the geographical specificity of the ancient Maori name, 'Land of the Long White Cloud', and the colonist's passion for combining the old country (the rich agricultural lands of the Dutch maritime provinces where Abel Tasman was born) with the indefinite expansionism of the New. The name articulates the dialectics of home and exile, harmony and expropriation, the clean and the destructive in these islands whose status as bicultural nation was born of the guerrilla victory of the Maori over the greatest army the world had ever known, and the treachery that stole their victory from them in the soon-dishonoured Treaty of Waitangi. That story of heroic warfare and betrayal is the common structure of myths of national origin, from the siege of Troy to King Arthur and Robin Hood, from Vercingetorix to the western. It is also the mythic structure of Tolkien's narrative, with the ironic difference that the only Maori players in the film appear in the helmets and prostheses of orcs and Uruk-hai villains. Yet the structure is the same: the heroic little people, outgunned and outnumbered, against the imperial evil. The films must operate, in the global marketplace, as generic myths of origin, rather than a tale specific to either England (Tolkien's desire) or Aotearoa. As if to ensure that generality, the film's extensive use of locations excludes perhaps the most iconic of all Aotearoa's landscapes: the sea shore, which appears only in the final sequence of the third film, and then in a studio-CGI composite based on the European paintings of Claude Lorrain and Turner. In short, Jackson's film does not depict these few South Pacific islands, but uses them as a springboard to picture a utopian and imaginary terrain forged – in every sense of the word – from the articulation of the local and the universal.

Like many small nations, Aotearoa New Zealand has diminishing power over its internal policies (Kelsey 1999). The limitations on sovereignty imposed by GATT (the General Agreement on Trade and Tariffs at the heart of the post-war global economy), international treaties binding countries to technological standards, legal norms and codes of diplomatic conduct, the necessity of offering tax breaks, restricting union power and providing infrastructure for inward investors all circumscribe the policy options open to governments. In an age where economic and political decision-making have been circumscribed or removed from its purview, the nation-state risks losing its legitimacy. It is not only 'rogue' states that risk policing by the wealthy nations. The cost of refusing to abide by norms established in international fora, not just political arenas like the UN but economic systems like the World Trade Organisation, is punitive. Few nations risk the wrath of the International Monetary Fund. And most must balance as best they can their aspirations for their citizens with the perceived necessity of bowing to the demands of investors. In this perplexity, a government or a state can lose its claim to legitimacy. But there is a zone of public life which is, within limits set by treaties on the trade in intellectual property, still open to governmental activity, and which offers both the possibility of growing new industries and claiming to serve the public good. For many nations, especially small nations, legitimacy now comes in the form of culture.

As in many other countries, film has been granted a special place in cultural policy, alongside public service broadcasting and the fine arts, and unlike more popular forms – games, sport, pop music, street fashion – which are treated as industries and rarely subsidised. And as in most other countries, there is no subsidy for the manufacture of film equipment, nor any sense that a film is any less a national product because it is shot on US cameras with German lenses. *The Lord of the Rings* films are a product of this uniquely local yet in many ways typical discourse of the era of globalisation. It is not just that government invested in the film, or that the national airline – again as in many countries a privileged site of state intervention – has decorated its planes with *Lord of the Rings* logos, playing, during 2003, a documentary guide to locations on all inbound flights. The film's success provided a site for a huge demonstration of popular support at the Wellington world premiere of *The Return of the King*, in festivitics reminiscent of major sporting victories. The third film's Oscar sweep (and host Billy Crystal's gags about the country) was likewise fêted as a source of patriotic jubilation. For Aotearoa New Zealand, still in the early 21st century largely a commodity-exporting, agrarian economy, the smokestack industries have made little dent. The extraordinary local economic impact of the films (New Zealand Institute of Economic Research, 2002) can be seen as indicating a unique path to development for the national economy, bypassing the manufacturing era to move straight to an information economy. Jackson's trilogy represents a major step in this direction, a company with basically a single product achieving an estimated turnover of $US1 billion, well over one per cent of the gross domestic product, US$74 billion in 2001. While New Zealanders looked to both tangible and expected economic benefits from the films' success, more was at stake: pride in a job well done and internationally recognised, both popularly and professionally esteemed. Both explicit and deep within this moment of exhilaration was a sense of the unique place the country had in the films' depiction of an ecotopia.

Pace the postmodern truism that nobody believes in grand narratives anymore (Lyotard 1984), eco-politics has become the single largest unifying political discourse of the early 21st century. Toby Miller and his collaborators (2001) argue that films cannot be understood solely in terms of their textual properties. Instead, those properties need to be addressed in terms that recognise the centrality of the global media industry to their production, their aesthetics and, one could add, to their technological standardisation. Nonetheless, despite their weakened position in the epoch of GATS (the General Agreement on the Trade in Services, an agreement which includes trade in creative product and intellectual property), nations still play a significant role, in cultural industries especially. In *The Lord of the Rings* we witness the interplay of patriotism and the requirements of globalisation: that contemporary big-budget films speak not only to the US box office but to the increasingly significant Asian market, a path most clearly marked in *The Matrix*'s mix of Hollywood action, Hong Kong fight choreography and Japanese graphic compositions. Though many, like Baz Luhrmann's Bollywood homage *Moulin Rouge*, shed all signs of their national origins, such cosmopolitan films need not do so, but they are constrained to construct scenarios and visual styles that will appeal globally. Global vernaculars of horror effects and comic book graphics have their place in *The Lord of the Rings*, but so too do the vernaculars of an emergent, worldwide political culture of anti-globalisation and ecology movements. What makes *The Lord of the Rings* significant in this context is that it balances the common fear of environmental Armageddon with the potentiality of a country in which it is still possible to imagine the green triumphant. Most of all, it comes from an increasing belief that through the development of highly technologised creative industries, it is possible to devise a mode of economic development that does not compromise the land.

Technologies of Middle Earth

Respect for boundaries is critical to the stability of Middle Earth, a respect mirroring the bio-security measures of the Department of Conservation (DOC), the environmental agency charged with protecting the island environments of Aotearoa New Zealand. The contradictions between communication and border patrolling, between the flow of trade, gifts and meanings on the one hand and the policing of biological integrity on the other (Clark 2002), structure the desecrations of Saruman in *The Lord of the Rings*, for example in the hybrid figures of the Uruk-Hai, all too easily legible as allegories of genetic modification and genetic engineering. In its imagining of Aotearoa New Zealand as Middle Earth, the films are in some senses closer to Hundertwasser, the Austrian environmentalist and artist who took Aotearoa to his heart, than to the influential but controversial phenomenologist of technology and nazi sympathiser Heidegger. For Hundertwasser, art, design and life were a single flow, and judgements about aesthetics indistinguishable from judgements of ecological efficiency. For Heidegger, on the other hand, 'the essence of technology is nothing technological' but is instead the act of diminishing the world by turning it into a mere means for attaining human goals. In the technological relation, not only does the world fade from its full presence, but humans too are diminished by their distance from it. Technology is then a symptom of a loss of being, a fading plenitude for which his entire philosophical works are a lament. Much of that nostalgic fatalism has found a home in poststructural thought, and much of it is echoed in contemporary green politics. But the *Lord of the Rings* films offer a richer and more future-oriented account of the relations between human, nature and technology than Heidegger's post-metaphysical metaphysics of lack, gaps and loss.

Design, craft and environment in harmony at Rivendell in *The Lord of the Rings: The Fellowship of the Ring.* Courtesy British Film Institute

Each of the peoples of Middle Earth inhabits a distinctive landscape. The soft rolling hills of Hobbiton are distinct from the dwarves' mountain fastness of Moria; the elves' woodland utopia Lothlorien is distinct from either the open moorlands of Rohan or the stone city of Gondor; while the anti-nature of Sauron is reflected in the fires and thorns of the desert of Mordor. Each habitat marks the crafts of each of the races, most apparent in the leaf motifs of the woodland elves, and the mallorn leaf which features strongly in the kidnap narrative of the second film. At the same time, among the most spectacular landscapes – notably the mountain ridges seen in helicopter shots evoking the magical forces at play in Middle Earth – are those which have no native people. In establishing shots of Hobbiton, Rivendell and Rohan, for example, the fit between culture and nature is celebrated in the harmony of design and environment. Beyond them lie landscapes which are sublime – the Southern Alps standing in for the Misty Mountains – or vile – the Dead Marshes for example. These inhuman landscapes reflect back on the populated realms of Middle Earth with the message that some environments refuse population. The habitable world is marked out as properly populated by their demarcation from worlds that are too lofty, or in some way forbidden.

One example of forbidden realms comes in the elimination of some backstory for the Balrog sequence. Mining has stood as symbolic of the end of the Golden Age throughout the European tradition. Lewis Mumford's modern revisitation and reaffirmation, 'One must admit the devastation of mining, even if one is prepared to justify the end', Mumford 1934:72 and passim), meets its contemporary reactivation in the Balrog. Tolkien is unambiguous: the Balrog has been awakened by the dwarves, because they have transgressed the unwritten law against delving too deep. In the film, however, the Balrog is just a force of nature, a mountain spirit, linked by colour thematic to Sauron's eye, otherwise unexplained. The cut absolves the dwarves of being the instruments responsible for the arrival of both teleological technology – mining for its own sake – and instrumental technology – the reduction of the mountain to a resource comprehended only what it represents, a source of wealth, rather than what it is. The monster is an ancient evil whose awakening is a matter of ill luck, but whose existence is as a cosmic force. Evil in this quasi-manichean universe is simple: an essence. The good, however, is complex, and faced with choices.

All Middle Earth's peoples are defined by their designs and their technologies, which stand in the film as the languages and their associated scripts do in the novel. These defining technologies, traits and techniques – horsemanship among the Rohirim for instance – are proper to each race and thereby both authenticated but also bounded, their mystery guarded like those of the mediaeval guilds and anchored in the spirit of place. At the same time these crafts are all communicative within and between communities, as garment, weapon or gift. The spatial boundaries dividing one territory of *The Lord of the Rings* from another also serve to distinguish the technologies of each of Middle Earth's races. A crucial distinction lies on the faultline between authenticity and inauthenticity, the border which the dwarves of Moria crossed when they awoke the Balrog. Authentic and inauthentic technologies of Middle Earth are marked by distinctive temporalities. The pleasures of Hobbiton are repeatable – pipeweed, ale – and the great artefacts, the Ring itself but also Sting, the mithryl shirt, Isildur's sword, are durable. Saruman's instrumental inventions on the other hand are ephemeral because self-consuming. Unlike the ancient monuments of Gondor, which may decay but still stand guard over the Falls of Rauros, Saruman's industrial plant can be washed away and destroyed in a day. The ecologically admirable species of Middle Earth use crafts: Saruman and Sauron are technologists. In their hands the earth is plundered, and those who wear Sauron's Ring find both the world and themselves diminished by that technology. In this sense, the film's seem to echo Heidegger's strictures on technology. But there are other forces in play.

The contradiction that makes the film so interesting is that it is a technological triumph in the service of a green mythology. The aim of the production design crew recounted throughout the DVD commentaries was verisimilitude, particularly to provide the various sets and locations with a sense of history. Entirely in keeping with the novels, this history is ingrained in the overgrown, used, broken and deserted. Likewise the actors wield their handtools and weapons with as much familiarity as possible, to give the viewer the sense of skills learnt not on the set but in the sinews. The designs of tools, architectures and

The rural, pre-technological pleasures of Hobbiton: *The Lord of the Rings: The Fellowship of the Ring.* Courtesy British Film Institute

weaponry speak of the 'long intersubjectivity' of Ricoeur and Gadamer, not least because production design has to stand in for the wealth of linguistic inventions that characterise the book and provide it with its melancholy sense of the fading of ancient civilisation. Yet insofar as it is marked as intersubjectivity, the temporality of each design family operates very precisely within geographically bounded regimes, so much so that their discovery beyond their own territories makes them evidence, like the fallen mallorn leaf brooches of the second film, and so objects distinguished from their environments, rather than elements of them. Their placedness is integral; travelling objects are evidence not only of alien intruders but of the breakdown of a 'natural' order of rooted location, a quasi-feudal anchorage in the turf of home.

Saruman's sin, for example, for which he is punished by Fangorn, is that he does not respect the *genius loci*. Aotearoa New Zealand shares with Australia a popular concern for the replacement of 'invasive' or introduced species with 'natives', paralleled in the European movements to rescue and restore lost species of fruit and livestock largely eradicated in agribusiness' drive to standardisation. Separated from Gondwanaland before mammals evolved, Aotearoa has only one native ground-dwelling bat and a scanty population of reptiles, but a rich and unique bird-life, and a range of trees, ferns and mushrooms that have evolved their own genera largely because of the absence of mammals or native bees. This unique ecology was first treated as wilderness by the European settler culture, tamed through the introduction of pastoral and dairy farming in particular, but it is now the object of extensive efforts to conserve, exactly, the genius loci, the unique spirit of the place. Assaults on the ecosystem of Aotearoa are popularly seen as twofold: introduced species and genetically modified species. Conservation, however, at times veers close to conservatism. A fiercely local commitment to conserving a unique ecology may also speak to a global (and indeed to an urban New Zealand) audience of a more sinisterly conservative cult of the Land.

This is why boundaries are so significant to the film. Clearly boundary crossing can happen: in the Fellowship itself, in the picaresque structure of the journey and most significantly in the added weight given by the films to the love between Arwen and Aragorn (with its comic parallel in the mateship between Legolas and Gimli). Otherwise matters of high seriousness, these interracial relationships are marked by duties, obligations, responsibilities and sacrifices, including the loss of community and of race-specific qualities (immortality), which must be deliberately chosen by an act of will in full knowledge of their consequences. It is at such junctures that the fear of contamination that belongs to the conservation movement meets the racism of the conservative protection of local culture. The strange absence of Maori from the re-imagined New Zealand of the films suggests that the culture to be protected is not that of the first inhabitants, but the civilisation of the Pakeha settlers. It is, in that instance, the imagination of a past that never existed, while it is also evidence of a dialectically fraught identification of the Pakeha settlers with the first inhabitants of the islands. The formality of relations between the various Middle Earth peoples, their reciprocal gifts and debts of honour, suggests a further complexity to the networks that both bind and divide them.

In certain respects the communicative universe of *The Lord of the Rings* is peculiarly premodern. In the 19th century, ladies could still view battles from adjacent hilltops, so tightly were the codes of battle limited to the professionals. At this stage war was 'narrowcast' in the sense that it was composed of a dialogue between defined sets of interlocutors and governed by codes that forbade the involvement of civilians. (Of course civilians suffered and were killed, but they were considered illegitimate victims, not collateral damage or intended targets, as they were at Dresden and Hiroshima, in Vietnam and Iraq). The age of narrowcast war ended somewhere between Sherman's March to the Sea and the bombing of Guernica during the Spanish Civil War. War is now a broadcast medium: as Hobsbawm notes (1994), 20th century wars were indifferent to the neutrality of civilians, who are statistically more likely victims than warriors in the conflicts of the early 21st century. Sauron's and Saruman's shame is that they wage modern war on enemies who uphold the chivalric distinction between soldiers and non-combatants. In the same way, Saruman's assaults on Fangorn Forest, the most direct images of environmental crime, are despicable because they broach a boundary between the permissible use and the impermissible waste of resource, to the point that the forest stops being a resource at all. In fact the model of war is applied to the forest as enemy, and one of the film's great moral satisfactions derives from the forest accepting that rôle and fighting back.

Like war, pollution has lost the bounded nature of its premodern occurrences. Industrial and population waste were at one time demarcators of class, intensely local to factories and the workers living in walking distance of them. But waste export, atmospheric pollution and global warming are broadcast. Skin cancer is no respecter of class or politics. Susan George points out that the transfer of industries to the *maquiladoras* sweatshops along the Mexican border has resulted in waste from factories and sewage travelling North back into the United States (George 1992: 26). Waste, in other words, is a mode of communication. It may be as natural as a gift – a child's gift of poo to its parent – or as counter-natural as the trade in nuclear detritus. It may be as conscious as the export of dirty industries or as unconscious as the use of deodorant sprays. Ecological science recognises that neither intention nor consciousness are requirements of communication – we communicate by virtue of our place in the network, by having a bank account or driving a car. Humans do not have to want to communicate by the medium of petroleum by-products or savings accounts, yet all unconscious as we are, those actions communicate through the medium of greenhouse gases and stock market fluctuations on the widest planetary scale. If there is a consciousness to such communications, it is global and transhuman, an ecological effect, not a quality of individual agents.

Similarly, the Elvish sixth sense that allows Galadriel to know in advance of the Fellowship's arrival is evidence of an ecological radiation of meaning and presence through the world. Nonetheless, even these unconscious communications can become tradable items, as in the US proposal for a world market in pollution credits allowing for the commodification of pollution. This is the meaning of the palantír , the Seeing Stone in Saruman's tower. Unlike Galadriel's ecologically networked vision, the palantír is a channel opened point-to-point, a narrowcast communication which has become, as we learn, a means for the delivery of moral pollution from Mordor to Isengard. Tolkien's backstory has not only more detail but a very different notion of the Stones. Of old, Gandalf tells Pippin, they were used 'To see far off, and to converse in thought . . . each *palantír* replied to each' (Tolkien 2001: 583-4). Like early cinematic accounts of television (*High Treason* [1927], *International House* [1932]), the Stones could see anywhere the viewer desired, and were to that extent an expression of a global environment that gave itself to vision. In the films, the palantír has lost that capacity (which is reserved, differently, for Galadriel's mirror) and become a medium of command, of a spectacle hiding a one-way commerce. The irony, once again, is that the films themselves, as products of a global media industry, deploy just such a one-way technology as the magical technologies that they criticise. The utopian claim for *The Lord of the Rings* depends on whether it can voice its own contradictions.

The Dialectics of Magic

The French eco-apocalyptic cycle (especially the films of Besson – *The Last Battle*, *Subway*, *The Fifth Element* – and Jeunet and Caro – *Delicatessen*, *The City of Lost Children*); Hollywood's eco-armageddons since *Soylent Green*, even the Australian *Mad Max* cycle share an ideological distrust of technology. In these movies and many more, military or industrial machines, implicitly or explicitly, have to bear the blame for the destruction of the green world. Worse still, such movies draw on a Romantic tradition stretching back through Emerson to Blake, in which machines and mechanistic thinking stand between the human and the green world, barriers to vision and to communication. Each proposes either fatalism or some route back to communion with nature through abjuring technology: sex in *The Fifth Element*, music in *Delicatessen*, dying in *Soylent Green*. What resolutions are possible involve returns, turnings back, a sometimes overpowering nostalgia for a past in which technology, impossibly, had no part in the relationship between humans and nature. What makes Jackson's films different is that they posit a possible resolution based on the very apparatus of illusion.

What is false, inauthentic, vile, amoral, anethical and an-aesthetic in *The Lord of the Rings* is manufacture – the smokestack industries. The good and true is craft – the craft of the armourer and the smith, the weaver, the sculptor and the brewer. Not just the artisan cultures that appear in the films, but likewise the smiths, armourers, weavers and sculptors who worked on the film belong to the good and the true. The same goes for the more contemporary guilds of the Director of Photography, editors, production designers and CGI crews. These guilds are organic in Goethe's sense: what they make is morphologically connected to its origins in the world. As the Elven brooch is to the mallorn leaf, so the cinematic sound-image is to Middle Earth. No-one would mistake the brooch for a real leaf. It is not evidence of the existence of leaves, nor does it serve as a semiotic index, pointing towards a specific individual leaf. Rather, the brooch's design grows out of the form of the leaf, which in-forms and shapes the artefact. This is the case with Middle Earth as imaged in the films: no-one believes that the films are evidence of its existence; nor does anyone expect that an image of Saruman's tower is an index of some real tower with an existence independent of its sign. Instead, the films stand as outgrowth, informed and shaped by the imaginary world, as the brooch is shaped by an imaginary tree. To the extent that the relationship is one of morphological informing, the two artefacts, brooch and film, participate in a broader natural process.

By contrast Saruman, Sauron and their technologies are de-naturing, as when greed for the Ring morphs Bilbo into a mask of snarling avarice at Rivendell. The crafts are organic in the Kantian sense that every part is an end in itself as well as an element of a totality. The dark magic is closer to Kant's definition of technology, determined externally, a hierarchy of parts subordinated to a purpose that is not its own and that overrides its elements in the interests of a planned use not otherwise inherent in the materials or the design.

Creating a binary opposition between organic craft and technological dark magic leaves us with a certain ambivalence about white magic and about Gandalf, who falls to the monster unleashed by the Faustian delvings of Moria. That the elision of the backstory of the Balrog's awakening is muted in the film has as effect to preserve the pride in craft of the miners' guild. The spectacular virtual set for the Great Hall of Moria does not have to be overshadowed by knowledge that its building called up nature's revenge on the dwarf technologists, and instead keeps them on the side of the guilds and the organic. Gandalf's guild is harder to analyse. The film softens and all but removes the Christian allegory so strong in the novel, especially in the resurrection of the Grey Pilgrim as Gandalf the White. Of course, the white wizard can be read allegorically as the figure of the filmmaker in the film, the weaver of spells, master of destinies, judge and guide. And like the filmmaker, he must work with nature rather than against it. Saruman and Sauron work against nature in their quest to control it. Their aim is to uproot the autonomy of the green world in order to reduce it to the status of Heideggerian standing-reserve, a mere pile of resources for purposes of which nature knows nothing. The white wizard, at the opposite end of the scale, is concerned to nurture a potential into existence, as he does most clearly in the scene of Frodo's moral education, when first we catch a glimpse of Gollum near the end of *The Fellowship*.

Two features of this sequence are noteworthy in this context, the shots of Gollum's fingerpads and eyes, the latter of which will feature so strongly in *The Two Towers*. Both are canonic indices of discrete individuality – fingerprints and retinal identification. Both are sensory and at the same time sensed, thresholds between inward and outward, telling as much as they learn. When later, in *The Two Towers*, we see him in full figure, the CGI creature serves to constitute Gollum as object. This first glimpse, however, establishes him as subject. Eyes and fingertips bring him into the networks of intersubjectivity which Gandalf notes in perhaps the most remarkable lines of dialogue in either novel or film: 'Many that live deserve to die, and many that die deserve life. Can you give it to them? Then do not be too hasty to give death'. What has removed him from those networks – and has damaged Bilbo and will damage Frodo – is the artefact of inwardness, the construction of self over and against the genus and the world. Gandalf's craft lies in sympathetic magic, fellow-feeling with Shadowfax or with the moth that brings the eagle to his rescue at Isengard – or with the despised Gollum. Contrast here the gradual construction of Frodo as object of the Nazgûl, an objectivity that both forces heroism upon him and deprives him of joy and freedom, other than the freedom to accept the quest. Wisdom then, as it occurs to Frodo, is an outside event that happens to him, a matter of loss. It is a loss he will bear on behalf of Middle Earth when the Elves depart and the age of magic will be over. The price of the defeat of manufacture is the loss of natural magic too. In their place there will remain only a human world. In this sense the trilogy moves towards the ending of illusion as narrative goal although its appeal lies strongly in the artifice of illusion. This sense of heroic destiny and heroic loss is characteristic of recent US hits, not least in the theme of undying love in James Cameron's *Abyss*, and *Titanic* and the Warchowski's *Matrix* cycle.

This triad of natural, instrumental and lost magic might be restated as a movement between physis, techne and polis. The polis is the social. Choosing this term rather than the more usual 'human' emphasises the Aristotelian concern with the *politikon zoon*, the social animal, a creature constituted in and by webs of support, trade, polity, language and belief. The Greek word techne carries more than technology: it includes craft, skill, practical knowledge, and embraces non-human crafts and knowledges as much as our own. Physis, in Dylan Thomas' beautiful definition 'The force that through the green fuse drives the flower', is the whole green world, not only Leopold's (2001) 'land', but the vital force itself, what we might today call evolution, which like polis and techne is not exclusive of humanity but embraces both human nature – the embodied, physical life we share with all organisms – and the power to evolve and adapt that characterises practical as well as technological knowledge. In a first moment, physis is in the films diametrically opposed to techne, the black arts of manufacture. And yet the human magic of information technologies, the technologies deployed in the construction of the film, announce themselves as resolving the disputation between green and iron. Their resolution, in which both will be transformed, lies in the human world of the polis, the restoration of the King in the fable of *The Lord of the Rings*, a new socio-cultural order derived from the marriage of technology and ecology celebrated in Jackson's Weta Workshops as a model not just for the creative industries but for the renewal of the whole national economy. Yet what makes this resolution so implausible is that it ignores the position of the films' making – and much more so their marketing – in an integrated global economy of exploitation and environmental degradation.

In the first film's most ambitious take, the minutes-long fly-through of the underground foundries of Saruman, the combination of digital, live-action and model work is integrated into a single vision of hell. It is in many ways a very daring shot. As Jackson notes on the extended version DVD commentary, the received wisdom is that model shots should be as brief as possible to avoid losing the illusion. And in an already long movie, to hold up the action while the camera indulges in spectacle is a risky manoeuvre in itself. But the shot works because it concentrates the ambivalence over technology. The vast anonymity of the factories should be placed opposite the intense individuation of Frodo in his scenes in Ring-space. In these scenes, beginning with the moment at which he first wears the Ring, at the Inn at Bree, Frodo is torn out of the world, isolated from his companions and from his environment, and reconstituted as the object of concentrated hatred and desire. At such moments, he is intensely objectified and identified, cornered, alienated, stripped of all meaning except for his task of carrying the Ring, and at the same time located as entirely individual, unique but also alone in being the object of Sauron's and the Nazgûls' scrutiny. Like the industrial worker of Lukacs (1971), he is in a single movement ripped from the world and placed back into it as the object of surveillance. Between the anonymity of modernity and the hyperindividuation of the postmodern micro-audience, target of so much individualised marketing effort, the proffered resolution of the polis stumbles. This is not a failing in the film but the realisation of its core thematic. The political world of the communicative creature, Aristotle's *politikon zoon*, may resolve one dialectic, but it is also the beginning of another.

Technology as Mediation

Was Tolkien a Heideggerian? Not by influence perhaps, but because both the Oxford don and the German philosopher derived their systems from a shared fascination with the etymologies of the Germanic (and in Tolkien's case the Celtic) languages? It may well be that both share, in Heidegger's phrase, a belief that 'Whatever stands by in the sense of standing-reserve no longer stands over against us as object' (Heidegger 1977: 17): that once the world is reduced to resource, it ceases to stand as a world in any emotionally satisfying sense of the word. At opposite ends of a spectrum, both Fangorn and the Balrog are autonomous of the human, and they stand over against the human as things that have their own presence. But their autonomy will end when the Elves leave Middle Earth, and the old things fade, as Heidegger writes of the fading of presence since the time of the pre-Socratics at the dawn of history. The autonomous presence of objects disappears, in Heidegger's later philosophy, as they cease to be apart from the human, and instead become a collection of tools and raw materials waiting to be fulfilled – and utterly changed – when they are used in human technologies. But in many ways, Tolkien's vision is less modern than Heidegger's, whose late works are grounded in the collapse of nazism and the post-war Germany of NATO and suburbanisation. It seems fair to say that Tolkien was more of a Kantian, sharing with the 18th century Sage of Königsberg a founding distinction between technology and the organic.

For Kant the internal logic of life combines parts into a unity such that 'an organised natural product is one in which every part is reciprocally both ends and means' (Kant 1952: 24), as opposed to the technological logic that subordinates parts hierarchically to the function of the whole.

When Hegel revised Kant's distinction decades into the 19th century, he emphasised the distinguishing factor as the internal logic of organic beings. In contrast to the organic, technological mechanisms are characterised by their 'external purposiveness' (Hegel 1969: 736): the *telos*, the first and final destiny of a knife, a saddle or a wagon is determined not by their parts, still less by any internal logic, but by the purpose they have for a user who is not a knife, a saddle or a wagon. Yet finally, that distinction arrives quite logically at Heidegger's principle, that 'the essence of technology is nothing technological' (Heidegger 1977: 35), because its essence is, in Hegel's terms, the consciousness of its fitness to purpose. Tolkien's trilogy shows a distinct distrust of the motives behind specific technologies, and of failure to observe the natural law against excess, while accepting the morphological principle that sees Hobbit technologies like watermills or Elvish technologies like weaving as wholly appropriate because their forms are so deeply determined by the nature and purposes of their makers.

A distinct question, and answer: is the Jackson movie Heideggerian? The answer is clearly no. Not just because the films' makers are so technologically proficient, but because this is, very explicitly, a world picture, something Heidegger hated as 'the making secure of the precedence of methodology over whatever is (nature or history)' (Heidegger 1977: 125). The films' designers clearly rejoice in the authenticity of artifice, the finality (*Zweckmaßigkeit*) of play. Against this authenticity – shared by the good folk of Middle Earth and the filmmakers, is ranged the inauthenticity of Saruman, and the counter-authenticity of Sauron. Between them lies the guild mystery of mining and metal craft, the craft of the dwarves. Where Hegel distinguished the external purposiveness of technology, Heidegger feared the arrival of a teleological technology, a technology whose own rationale would lead it towards a conquest of the world. Tolkien perhaps shared this fear, albeit in the Romantic tradition of Blake and Ruskin. But in the films, the fear is shifted, made more subtle, in order to accommodate the intrinsically technological dimension of the film's making, and in deference to the changing nature of our technologies.

According to the French philosopher Jean-François Lyotard, 'By sacrificing itself, the imagination sacrifices nature, which is aesthetically sacred, in order to exalt holy law' (Lyotard 1994: 189). In sacrificing its own freedom, imagination achieves the freedom of the law, but in doing so, and in so becoming more purely human, imagination must give up its otherwise intrinsic links to the natural world. . The link between nature and imagination as it functions in *The Lord of the Rings* is the work of natural magic. The fading of the Elves is the sacrifice that allows for the emergence of Men, the polis of laws. The cost of this transition is the hyperindividuation which Frodo suffers. The commodification of attention and its delivery as proletarianised consumption demands the construction of just such an obsessively determined subjectivity as Frodo falls into every time he wears the Ring – subjectivity as an affliction of instrumental technology. In that movement, the world becomes Other, and the option of immersion in it is removed from the magical to the informatic. There can be no healing bath of nature, but there is the balm of the loss of subjectivity in the embrace of this cycle of films, and beyond them in the vast ocean of human communication. The special effects technologies so skilfully deployed stand not only for Middle Earth but for themselves, as crafts of mundane, rule-governed magic. That they are also fallen, imbricated without possibility of redemption in the global nets of the commodity, marks them out as the internally conflictual harbingers of the new dialectic of the new commodity: between the manufacture of sign value and the discipline of consumer attention. The utopian dimensions of the film are less about a green world untouched by technologies than about the possibility of a post-commodity communication in which techne and physis are embraced in the polis.

What the first two films establish, the third breaks down. In *The Fellowship* and *The Two Towers*, there is a determined effort to establish the distinction between the realms of Middle Earth, through remnants of their languages (of which only Elvish retains any prominence in spoken form, though Mordor, Dwarves and Hobbits have distinctive scripts) but especially in the coherence of design. *The Return of the King* adds the gothic romanesque of Gondor to the repertoire, a style echoed in the architecture of the Grey Havens in the final scenes. Drawing on Claude Lorrain's *Embarkation of Sheba* and Turner's *Dido Leaving Carthage*, both in the National Gallery in London, the architecture differs from the classicism of its source paintings in the rounded arches, domes and elongated statuary of Gondor romanesque. The preserved Shire too keeps its distinctive style, in the round doorway whose closing marks the completion of the trilogy. And yet the departure of Gandalf and the elves marks too the softening of borders between the races. The celebration of Aragorn's coronation, and Frodo's awakening after the destruction of the Ring, both feature an admixture of the realms, many like the pairing of Faramir and Eowyn without authority from the source in Tolkien. This reiteration of alliance and hybridity does more than shift the balance from loss in Tolkien towards a futurity symbolised by children, notably Arwen's vision of a child she will bear to Aragorn. The departure of the elves establishes the ground for a new order. In this order, the absolutes of good and evil marked by the elves and Sauron are no longer the governing powers. Despite persistent rumours, the omission of the penultimate drama of the books, the Cleansing of the Shire from the extended version of *The Return of the King* continues the move away from Tolkien's Romantic disapproval of technology. Instead, the scene at the Grey Havens affords a final triumph of artifice.

An emblematic sequence from the final film is the lighting of the beacons. Pippin's scramble up the pyre – pre-echo of the pyre on which Denethor will place his son – is caught in cuts between hand-held close-ups and points-of-view and more controlled crane-shots for the wide angles, with cutaways to unusually static midshots of Gandalf trying to look inconspicuous. But once the beacon of Minas Tirith is aflame, we move into an ambitious composite with flamboyant circling camerawork. A few shots later, there is an elegantly composed and very gently reframed point-of-view balancing the back of Gandalf's head screen left with his staff bisecting a CGI dome screen right, a line of mountains leading diagonally away centre to lead the eye towards the tiny spark of a distant hilltop beacon flaring. There follow six elaborate helicopter shots of the Southern Alps with live-action and virtual beacons lighting up until we reach another elegantly asymmetric shot of Aragorn catching sight of the flame on an adjacent mountaintop. Though Gandalf provides a jubilant audience, the fictional technology of the signal fires is entirely human, entirely non-magical. Yet it is just the kind of magic to earn the emblematic disapproval of the scowling hobbit reprised from the opening of the first film at the close of the third. And it is depicted using very powerful technologies that denature the spectacle, even as they rejoice in the cloud-shrouded and snow-peaked mountains. The human and the natural here combine through that third force which, in Tolkien, was without redeeming features beyond brewing, handcraft and the watermill. In this sequence, imagined ancient communication technology is depicted through vibrantly contemporary communications of transport and representation.

The inference for all the films is that technology has a unique position in mediating between the human world and the natural. We might in this instance then rewrite Lyotard's imagery of the sacrifice of natural imagination to holy law, and suggest that through techne, physis can address the human not as bare life but specifically as polis, as society of communicating agents, or more powerfully still as agents formed in networks of communication which are indifferently technological or natural. Perhaps this explains the satisfying structure of the shot of Aragorn, sipping from a bowl outside an old barn, where a half-made wheel stands propped against the wall. In place of Tolkien's mood of regret there is a dawning consciousness that such rough technologies as wagon wheels contain the beginnings of a different relation between human and nature, one that does not so much sacrifice nature to law as articulate physis and polis. Polis, then, is not the imposition of law or sacrifice to it, but the dawning awareness that commerce, in all senses of the word, demands not only socialisation – and so a sacrifice of the brutality of bare, asocial survival pitted against nature – in favour of networks of communication that will shape and transform human and natural alike in the lens of their mutual approach in the forms of techne.

Fangorn, of all creatures in the trilogy, seems to embody this strange hinterland. In Tolkien, Treebeard belongs to the ancient days, and he speaks for what might today be accounted a deep ecology: an absolute valuation of the green world as a world apart. Yet here he is assembled as a combination of animatronics and computer-generated effects, and with a voice modulated both before recording (Rhys-Davis spoke his lines through a specially-constructed wooden box to secure a suitably woody tone) and in post-production, and frequently seen in shots in which real branches and leaves have been brought into a studio, as well as composited with location footage of real bush. One of Tolkien's most compelling creations, Fangorn is able to speak on behalf of the green world only because he *can* speak, that is, to the extent that he partakes of the polis. In the films, this communication is made more explicitly dialectical: Treebeard speaks, moves, emotes on behalf of the forest only because he is a construct of technology, just as Tolkien's was a construct of words. Yet words always seem, despite the critical literature to the contrary, far more transparent than highly technologised special effects cinema, where the construction of the image is never absent from the image itself. Like the Balrog under the mountain, Fangorn is an ancient spirit, from before the days of the polis. But before the polis, there was no physis distinct from it: when humans were still animal, how could they distinguish themselves from their world? What Fangorn in the films affords is a glimpse of what may yet occur between the two terms, polis and physis, once torn apart – that they engender a new term, techne, in which their sundering, which can never be undone, can nonetheless produce a new kind of relationship, a new mediation, that was impossible when the two were one. Kant's old distinction between technology and organism here breaks down: as mediation, techne is both ends and means, a relationship, or network of relationships, unstill and ever-changing, between the unstill and ever changing partners, physis and polis, which it both distinguishes and articulates. Reconceived in the aesthetic moment of cinema, where technology is at its most utopian, the logic of techne looks far more like the logic of life.

Drawing Animals

Zoomorphism in Princess Mononoke

The creatures outside looked from pig to man, and from man to pig, and from pig to man again; but already it was impossible to say which was which. (Orwell, *Animal Farm* 1951: 120)

The Return of the Repressed Environment

The work of natural magic in articulating polis and physis, the work of its self-renunciation, and the toll which that work extracts in hyperindividuation, are not historical events like the signing of an armistice. They are processes that tend not to complete themselves, that people are drawn to over and over again. Clearly there can be no articulating distinct realms of being until they have been sundered, and yet that act of tearing the human and the biological apart is not an action that is ever successfully completed. Of course we carry in us the biology of mammals and our symbiotes and parasites. To distinguish human from animal is thus also to establish a fluctuating frontier somewhere within the human, between angel and brute, mind and body, instinct and drive, nature and nurture, sex and gender. That internal border zone, shifting and uncertain as it is, nonetheless defines the external limit between humans and animals. Our fascination with animals belongs to this deep uncertainty about ourselves, and underpins the work of making cartoon depictions of the creatures with whom we share our world and to some unstill degree our nature.

Not purely for etymological reasons, animation likes animals. From Gertie the Dinosaur to Nemo the clown fish, cartoons have repeatedly returned to the image of the finned, the feathered and the furry. The relationship is so deeply intertwined we scarcely notice, a sure sign of an enquiry waiting to be made. In these days of BSE, chicken flu and species extinction, our relationships with animals have reached a pitch of intensity that animations articulate. Difference and continuity between the two phyla fascinate films, especially cartoons. What is it that they are trying to tell us?

After Freud and Darwin, it is difficult to say where being animal stops and being human begins. The religious distinction that provided humankind with souls but left the animals without has faded in the secular light of science, and even the religious find it hard to accept unnecessary cruelty to animals. But then, where do we draw the line? Do we have to be kind to mammals, allow neutrality towards reptiles, but permit ourselves to be thoughtless towards insects? Distinctions based on language are equally vague: the higher primates and marine mammals, those favourites of the movies, are joined by at least some domestic animals, notably dogs, among the communicative species. But then the complex communications of songbirds and honeybees, alien though they are and open to all sorts of non-linguistic explanations, all the same overcome us with their proximity to speech. Tool-using apes, even the secretary bird that taps at eggshells with a stone, not to mention the architectures of bower birds and termites or fungi-farming ants, soften the edges that distinguish *homo faber* from the birds of the field that reap not, neither do they sow.

And we humans appear to ourselves from time to time as 'nasty, brutish and short', when hooligans are described as 'animals' or we call each other 'chicken', 'slug', or 'pig', or describe one another as feline, aquiline or bovine. The animal passions threaten to overwhelm reason; in dire extremity animal needs supersede politics; and not even animal spirits can keep us cheerful. Today we describe as bestial those who once treated slaves, first peoples, Jews and Romanies like animals, as if both parties, at different moments, lacked some defining characteristic of language, freedom, reason or morals to mark them off from the beasts. The boundaries are marked not just with social regulations but with physical disgust at the thought of eating the unclean – animals that live among human waste for example – or too human by association: domestic animals and primates, chief among which of course are humans themselves. Yet equally clearly some of us eat shellfish, amphibians, reptiles, insects and gastropods while revolted by the thought of some certain mammals finding their way to the dinner table. Boundaries within the animal kingdom and between it and the human are indistinct, and yet, as Agamben (2004) argues, fundamental to definitions of what 'human' means. Hitchcock's famous *bon mot* to the effect that 'actors are cattle' can of course be turned on its head: sometimes cattle are actors, at least in the Western, and even more frequently other creatures feature. Again, the boundaries blur, for example in Viggo Mortenson's relation with the horse Brega which, as Aragorn, he tames in the stables of Rohan, and which the actor subsequently bought. The $4 million dollar programme to look after Keiko, the orca who played the lead in *Free Willy* (http://www.keiko.com/history.html), also points towards a blurring of modality between spectacle and actuality, far stronger in the case of live-action performers than other kinds of animals.

But despite the long history of animal performers, from *Rescued By Rover* to *Babe*, it is in the animated film that animals have come to take their strongest position in the media. Drawn images of animals are among the first records that distinguish the presence of humans. Vilém Flusser goes so far as to argue that

> Man's unique ability to create images for himself and for others has been a theme of philosophical and theological speculation at least since Plato. This ability seems truly unique to man, because none of the species preceding him seem to have created anything comparable to images such as the cave paintings in Dordogne (Flusser 2002: 110).

As Flusser goes on to note, Plato was not alone in despising this talent. If indeed the making of images distinguishes humans from beasts, it is at least an oddity that God dislikes the practice enough to ban it outright in the religions of the book. Something sacrilegious is involved. For Plato, since the phenomenal world was a shadow of the ideal forms, a picture of the phenomenal world was a shadow's shadow, an *eidolon* that lost contact with its original, a simulation. For Moses and the Prophet, God alone reserved the right of creation. If Man was made in God's image, to make an image of Man was to usurp or to pervert God's creative singularity. Alternatively, for the Christian iconoclasts, the image stood between human and divine. Instead of worshipping God, people would worship images, the sin of iconolatry. And perhaps some of that distrust of images which Martin Jay (1993) traces in French theory of the 20th century has some of its roots in the same tradition.

How strange, that this potentially unique human facility should be so deeply suspect, and at a time when, according to scholars like Flusser, the image is returning to supremacy after the end of the era of the written word. In the essay 'Line and Surface', Flusser argues that the linear and causal model of writing, which defined history as distinct from image-based pre-history, was challenged by the arrival of a new, mythic, spatialising image, just at that moment when universal literacy seemed ready to democratise historical consciousness. But the new image is not the same as the old – there is no chance that 'illiteracy will be restored' (Flusser 2002: 67). Instead we have to understand the technical image as a new form. Where prehistoric images attempted a magical translation of the world, the new images process pre-existing linear texts. Our images (and their apparatuses) are created from scientific formulae, philosophical arguments, historical narratives. But they process them into second-order images, if anything even more removed from the world than the texts they supplant. One thinks here of Feynman diagrams or Penrose tiles – images that visualise complex multidimensional math. These 'post-historical' images take us neither to Fukuyama's (1992) triumphant neoliberalism, nor to McLuhan's (1989) neo-pre-literate global village but to a zone where the ethics of criticism become indistinguishable from the crisis of freedom and the new modes of politics that ensue.

If it distinguishes the human, why should drawing, especially in its animated form, be so regularly and powerfully attracted to the drawing of that from which it distinguishes the designer: animals? Giorgio Agamben, in his short, dense work on the various ways philosophy has attempted to distinguish between animal and human and how it has consistently failed, suggests that

> In our culture man has always been the result of a simultaneous division and articulation of the animal and the human in which one of the two terms of the operation was also what was at stake in it. To render inoperative the machine that governs our conception of man will therefore mean no longer to seek new – more efficient or more authentic – articulations, but rather to show the central emptiness, the hiatus that – within man – separates man and animal. and to risk ourselves in this emptiness: the suspension of the suspension, Shabbat of both animal and man (Agamben 2002: 92).

Western philosophy has consistently tried to define each term (animal, human) in terms of the other, as distinct. This process he refers to as the anthropogenic machine, a logical process which generates human-ness out of the distinction from animality, a machine which however never works. Instead, he argues, there is a gap *within* the human creature where the difference is both generated and denied, a gap which could become the basis for a philosophy which is not based on separation (and, he notes approvingly, which would not be based on the exclusively human task of making history). With varying degrees of playfulness and seriousness, drawing animals is an exploration of this gap.

But where Agamben sees a nothingness, drawing is a positively generative process. Agamben sees a vanishing point where for the activity of drawing there is a moment of becoming. Traditional theories of perspective (and of the technical function of camera and projector lenses and the optical properties of the human eye) see vision as a series of vanishing points. But from the standpoint of drawing and animation these same points where rays of light cross over one another are generative moments. Instead of conceiving of vision as a series of disappearances, we can reconceive it as a series of emergences into the light, moments of becoming visible, transitions from nullity into space and time. The nodes of lens, screen and eye are moments that transform and reorient the world and its observers into new relationships. To the extent that these processes are physical and physiological, they belong as closely to the animal as to the human. But there may be a sense in which at least some of these 'moments of becoming' are peculiar to human drawing, in the sense that drawing generates space, and more generally dimensionality – as when a represented space becomes navigable, like the caves, like the Stations of the Cross, or like narrative paintings.

So that, while it is tempting to accept Flusser's observation that humans draw and animals do not, it is worth pausing over the ways that animals might be said to draw, or at least to draw attention to themselves. My dog, like pretty much all dogs, marks her territory with scent. You could say that she is drawing a boundary or a map. But in this case, the map that is the same size as the territory doesn't disguise and displace the ground. Instead it is inextricable from the ground. This would suggest that what distinguishes human drawing is the severance of figure from ground. Among the earlier petroglyphs are several that are modifications of the rock face, improvisations on existing formations (Leroi-Gourhan 1986), like make-up on a face. Here the distinction is not so powerful, and the continuities with territorial marking stronger, a trait that remains with even the most mobile of logos as an element of human space-making. The discontinuity seems instead to arise when the drawing can be lifted, either mentally or physically, from its environment, when it occupies a space other than the surface on which it is marked. Moreover, the drawing is something new, something that has a beginning in time, as a territory does not for the dog that marks it. In this sense the act of drawing marks a moment of becoming (a process that is read in reverse when geometric inspiration redefines it as vanishing point). Animals are capable of signifying through a gesture, which is a combination of matter and energy. What they do not appear to do is to gift their marks with dimensionality, with space and time. That, it appears, is the prerogative of human drawing.

The dimensional properties of drawings, the way they occupy space and time in ways different to the territory they are marked on, distinguishes them from the meaningful gestures of animals, even while the notion of a meaningful gesture remains as evidence of a continuity between the two. This in turn may help to understand why God dislikes drawing so: it embraces both the continuity with animals and, in its deployment of space and time as raw materials, it leaps towards godhead. So drawing risks eliminating the human as a distinct zone between creator and creature. Which in turn may suggest why animators like animals: because in drawing them we pass strangely close to the divine, while at the same time flirting with animality through the kind of identification that you feel when drawing, perhaps some remnant of that identification with prey animals we can imagine among the cave painters. Perhaps God dislikes drawings of his creatures because, in the act of drawing, it is all too easy to be possessed by their spirits.

'The role of the mind has been vastly exaggerated, as has that of perception', notes Bruno Latour. 'An average mind or an average man, with the same perceptual abilities, within normal social conditions, will generate totally different output depending on whether his or her average skills apply to the confusing world or to inscriptions' (Latour 1998: 47). The mind is not in itself a strong enough marker of difference, between people or between human and animal. What counts in the development of science, Latour's subject, is the skill with which intelligence and observation are applied not so much to the external world as to the marks we make as we assemble data about it. Latour's focus in the essay just cited lies in the relationships between visualisation techniques, the printing press and the emergence of modern science. But the observation holds good of the process of drawing animals. Any mark distinguishes, and any line that forms a boundary encloses one space and excludes another. The skill of drawing defines the drawn as distinct from its activities and its environment. As the drawing distinguishes itself from the surface it is drawn upon, so it demarcates the space occupied by the drawn animal from the rest of the world. Thus simplified, abstracted from its unpredictable process of living and its unruly and unthinkable complexity of detail, it can become an object of knowledge, and perhaps control. But while this description may be true of scientific drawing, it does not tell the whole tale of the cartoon animal, which also has the task of describing the connection as well as the distinction between the viewer and the drawing.

Zoomorphism

The extent to which the child is permitted to be animal-like is strictly circumscribed. Little angels, little devils, little monsters, children have to be lead away from instinct and towards mastery, the mastery of objects, including themselves as bodies, and to that extent mastery over animals as objects. This is the process of internalising the chiasmus of Agamben's anthropogenic machine, the systems of self-awareness which will, constantly revising and rewriting the distinction, generate the humanness of the human being out of the difference from animality. The problem the child faces at this juncture is not that of the other, animal or machine, but of distinguishing a social self, of identifying with its own species. However permeable the membrane separating animal and human, body and mind, in the infant, some line must be drawn so that the child can become part of society. The function of animals, especially perhaps in an urban culture, is to allow the child to recognise what distinguishes the one from the other, not at first internally but as each can be perceived in the other. The process of identification however, once started, cannot be stopped. Having acquired a human identity emphasising identification with other humans, the child does not cease to identify with other others, less human, more animal. No relation to the 'becoming-animal' of Deleuze and Guattari (1980: 284-380), this is a process that predates it, a distinction on which their determined ascent towards animality as the ultimate other is premised. Framed in antipathy to companionate animals, Deleuze and Guattari's becoming animal requires this premise of absolute distinction between human and animal to operate. But what we learn from drawing animals is that the opposition is by no means as clear cut as they believe, and need to believe if their approach to wild humanity is to work. In cartoons we must face up to the fact that there is nothing so human as identification across species.

Tracing the outline of an animal – cartooning – is perpetually inadequate as representation or depiction but nonetheless attuned to some basic requirement of being human. In childhood, we need to acquire the skills of (re)cognising, acquiring some kind of fellow-feeling. Cartooning (a kind of distorting-mirror phase) permits trans-species identification that a photographic image, evidence of alienness, would not allow. Moreover, as Lippit (2000: 173) notes, 'A direct relation between the nature of the photograph and that of the animal resides in the look – a look without subjectivity – that both media project'. Photographs of animals translate the unanswerable gaze of a fellow creature as though it lacked a soul, its implication for the child being that it too is a creature without subjectivity. But that is exactly what it is the task of depicted animals to supply: an other subjectivity, not an absence. Cartoon animals like the Lion King, Dumbo or Bambi are sufficiently human-like for the child to enjoy without fear (and sufficiently neotenic for the adult to reconcile them as childlike and therefore appropriate companions for their offspring). With creations like *Bambi*, Disney abandoned the free play of the line in favour of the aesthetic of constant volume and bounded surfaces. More coherent and more consistent with reality than their fantastic forebears like Felix the Cat, these animals were closer to the stuffed toys that began to fill children's bedrooms in the 19th century: safe and infantile companions for the very young, somehow younger even than themselves, on whom the child might practice caring, or indeed violence, without responsibility. The animals themselves disappeared under the blanket of messages they were burdened with teaching to the young. Older and crueller tales of wolves gave way to cuddly tales of teenage lions. And yet the alienness of the animal remains, and with it the sense that the control that knowledge brings is always uncertain, always at the mercy of the division that at once separates and conjoins the social mind and the natural body. Drawing animals is a constant traverse to and fro across that divide, at some moments a suture, at others the oscillations of an unstable wave.

'Anthropomorphism', writes John Berger, 'was the residue of the continuous use of animal metaphor. In the last two centuries, animals have gradually disappeared. Today we live without them. And in this new solitude, anthropomorphism makes us doubly uneasy' (Berger, 1980:9). For Berger a natural bond has been broken for the majority of Westerners who no longer live in proximity to animals. The household pet, he argues, is a last, denatured link to that old world. Commenting on this essay, Esther Leslie notes that Berger's golden age resolves into an image of a time when people had to rely on animals and so had to respect them. She cites against Berger a radio talk by Walter Benjamin, 'True Stories About Dogs':

> For thousands of years, Benjamin insists, dog has been slave and man master. But man's victory is not absolute, and dogs retain traces of their untamed and self-sufficient origin. Caught between wolfish past and devotion to humans, the dog straddles the line between nature (animality) and culture (humankind). The dog is dialectical (Leslie 2002: 243).

The anthropomorphic retains its power, though the species (*Antz*, *A Bug's Life*, *Finding Nemo*) are less like furry toys today, and *Nemo* contains a moral fable against removing reef fish from their habitats. Animations do in general impose a human face on the animal world. Yet not only the household pet but even the animated fish retain some remembrance of another, wilder life, and remain dialectical, like Benjamin's dog. The thoroughly technologised medium of animation, however, adds another layer of enquiry into the distinctions between organic and technological, distinguishing not only human from animal but both from machines. Tales of cross-species alliances abound in the form of moral fables. But even when these are as anthropocentric as *Antz*, the estrangement effect of reconfiguring human neuroses and human politics among species for whom they are clearly irrelevant says something back to the presumption that the anthropic principle rules the whole process of the film. The boundaries still have power, but the narrative is the tale of their transgression, and so an account of demarcations but also of responsibilities across the border. Identification is thus extended beyond mere empathy into a realm where the relationship is transgressed not by the projection of human qualities onto anthropomorphised animals, but by the introjection of animal properties into the spectator: the process of zoomorphism.

Possession

Anime are potentially shocking because they break the North American codes of neoteny, and allow the doe-eyed heroes and heroines to face and perpetrate adult and animal cruelty and violence. Their aesthetic is less about the anthropogenic or the curiously distanced and irresponsible care of the child for the stuffed toy, and more about possession: possession of the animal by the human, certainly, but also of the human by the animal, and of both by other agencies. As is the case of '*mononoke hime*', the possessed princess, heroine of Japan's biggest grossing movie, the anime *Princess Mononoke*. The film is set in the 14th century Muromachi period, into which, anachronistically, the indigenous Emishi, otherwise destroyed in the 8th century, have survived. Ashitake, scion of the royal family, is out in the forest when the village is menaced by a *tatari gami*, a 'curse god' or god of vengeance, the transformed shape, it transpires, of a wild boar god poisoned by an iron bullet. Blighted in his turn, Ashitake must set off on a quest to discover the source of the boar god's wound. On the road he encounters

San, the possessed princess of the title, who walks between human and animal kingdoms as the ward of the wolf god. War breaks out between technologists (the ironworkers), greedy samurai hoping to get their hands on the iron, the Emperor's stooge entrusted with the task of bringing him the head of the forest spirit, source of immortality, and the factional but commonly angry gods of the forest. The love of Ashitake and San provides the basis for a resolution based on the reconciliation of technology and woodland.

The relationship between technology and nature appears stylistically in the opening sequence. The *tatari gami* is covered in a forest of something between flames, worms and distended blood vessels, powerfully ugly. Much of this was rendered in CGI before being parsed in Toonshader, a product developed by the film's producer, Ghibli Studio, in partnership with Microsoft's Softimage subsidiary, to give CGI images a more cel-like shallowness and colour range. We confront here a third order of drawing, the technological. Technological drawing does not add anything new to drawing technique, but rather eliminates one moment of it: the gesture. Though technically speaking digital artists will frequently use tablets and light-pens to input lines, the significant loss is the trace of the raw gesture itself, the auratic trace that marks the presence of a making hand: the gesture that begins the process of digital animation is rapidly transformed into an array of numbers, any one of which can be modulated in the software. The hand is removed from the drawing.

The loss of gesture, and the consequent emphasis on dimensionality and significance, marks off the technological image not so much from the human as from the animal, where gesture and meaning are inseparable. In this form of technical image, everything resides in the spatio-temporal array of data in computer storage. The gesture is replaced by a distribution of anchor points in a three dimensional matrix, automating the assembly-line method of key-framing, in which lower-grade 'in-betweeners' supply the step-frames articulating two still keyframes supplied by the lead animator. Writing about early typewriters, Friedrich Kittler (1999) observes that replacing copperplate orthography with distinct keystrokes resulted in the fragmentation of written language into signifiers, divided writing off from the voice, the hand and from the continuities of speech and gesture. In a similar fashion, the mechanisation of drawing works by fragmenting movement into discrete cels. By eliminating the gesture, by automating it as a bitmap of points or a mathematical function of vector graphics, the continuity of hand and eye is disrupted. In place of a gesture traced directly on a surface, digital drawing records the mark as a spatio-temporal array of points or an array of objects in computer memory. The figure-ground relation that first distinguished human drawing is extended to the point that drawing is no longer directly articulated with the surface on which

San, the possessed princess of the title, rides her adopted mother the wolf god through the threatened forests of *Princess Mononoke.* Courtesy British Film Institute

it is recorded: a digital drawing exists only in the computer, but it can be realised on anything you care to print it on. Like writing in the age of the typewriter, animated movement becomes not only particulate, but seems to lose its physical grounding in the world. In one sense then we can read the curse laid on the boar god as the technological divorce of the mode of his representation from the ways in which he himself, as territorial animal, uses the gesture of laying scent to draw his map. The technological wound – the bullet – denatures even a god, and leaves him ravening for revenge on the humans who introduced the technological into his natural world, and in so doing abstracted him from his gestural physics to this dimensional grid of flame and suppuration.

In this vein, then, Ashitake's quest will be to reconcile the gestural with the technical, the physical and the dimensional. In the process, the forest spirit who embodies the cycle of life and death has to be sacrificed. Here we meet a similar stylistic expression of the technical/natural division, for the forest spirit has two forms, a daylight form as a kind of elk, and a night-time form as a stellar and fantastic creature bestriding the hills. The former is drawn in the usual anime style, but the latter, the nightwalker, is a composite of animation and digital effects. The apocalyptic moment of the beheading occurs at the very moment of transformation from the elk form to the nightwalker, from animation to digital drawing. Beheaded, the forest spirit becomes entirely CGI, a star-flecked and amorphous body of darkness pouring a tide of death over the landscape, destroying forest and foundry alike. Only when reunited with its head can it die, and life return to the forest. Ashitake's quest involves overcoming the rage of the wounded creature, 'to see with eyes unclouded by hate'. Like Neo in the final scenes of *Matrix Revolutions*, his task is to reconcile the irreconcilable, here the forest with Irontown, as there Zion with the machine city. The technological image operates in both films to mediate this inter- (and implicitly intra-) species gap. In *Matrix Revolutions*, the blind Neo sees the machine city as pure special effect. In *Mononoke*, Ashitake sees the spectacle of the dying god, whose death returns green shoots to the wrecked hillsides and even cures the leper blacksmiths of Irontown. Lady Eboshi will build a better town, with Ashitake promising both to help rebuild and to maintain his relationship with San, and through her with the green world. The mutual hatred of human and animal, iron and green worlds is to be reconciled, through the ministry of an order that is neither human nor wild but entirely technological. Since this rebuilt world is implicitly one which renounces progress, its time is cyclical and its space finite. A kind of cyborg supernature, the dying CGI god marks the passage from history into myth, from linear to circular, from abstraction back to the ground and round again. Unlike *The Matrix* trilogy, *Mononoke* doesn't promise a final truce but an undeterminable repetition. The only alternatives would be either the victory of the forest and the end of humans, or the victory of progress: either no time at all, or a linear time of destruction.

There is a double motion in our relationship with drawn animals. On the one hand, there is the projection into the animal, the attempt to feel what it is to be animal. And on the other, there is the introjection of the animal in contemplation, the way we draw animality into ourselves when drawing or otherwise contemplating a living animal. Mad Nietzsche embracing the flogged horse was perhaps over-effusive, but typical. That moment of heartfelt empathy across the special gap was also perhaps a painting of the beaten horse in the colours of Nietzsche's own despair. The wounded beast-gods of *Mononoke* are sites for such doublings of anthropomorphic projection and zoomorphic introjection. They are like us in order that we should have the chance to become like them. But the trajectory of *Mononoke*'s fable appears to be that the only reconciliation possible requires the mediation of an extra-human, demonic in the first instance, divine in the last, which is purely technological – purely, that is, in the sense that the technological abstracts itself from the physical world of matter and energy, of the gesture, so that space and time alone signify. It is as if, in the problematic gap between the human and the animal, that same gap that lies within and without, and which the sight of suffering brings so close, there is generated a new relation. This is the technological image characterised by its abandonment of physics in favour of dimensionality and a homeostasis composed of a circular orbit between life and death. Neither projection nor introjection, to the extent that it is extracted from matter and energy, we might call this the moment of extrojection, a propulsion out of the physical into a domain of pattern.

The spirit of the forest in his elk form before his transformation in *Princess Mononoke.* Courtesy British Film Institute

This extrojected image is both demonic and divine, beneath and above the organic, because it creates an image, not of the phenomenon, but of the idea of the phenomenon. Like scientific knowledge, in its orchestrated form of professional discourse and protocols for imaging and visualisation, the extrojected image is particulate but not particular. It pictures a state of things otherwise beyond depiction, in the same way that 'the economy' or 'the electromagnetic spectrum' are not visible, but can be visualised. Viewed in this perspective, the fall of the visualised god is the necessary prerequisite for the return of a green world. The life-force, if it exists, cannot be summed as a single deity, no matter how vast. Extrojected from the world, it is alien to the world, and a danger to it. Ripping head from body and reassembling them to enable the necessary death might then smack of a parable about embodiment and rationalism, except that the union of the two is fatal to the deity, albeit fertile for the world.

When an animal 'draws', when we draw an animal, or when a machine produces a drawing of an animal, the processes are all significant, but occupy different modes of existence. For an animal, a drawing is a technique that gives gesture, an arrangement of matter, meaning. Human drawing clearly does this too, but in addition organises the drawing in space and time in such a way that it attains the status of an object, something discrete, separable from the physical mark, and significant because it distinguishes the physical from the dimensional properties. For the machine, the trajectory is from dimensionality to significance, an axis which can be characterised as economic, in the sense that it organises information in space and time, but also produces, information out of the ordering of dimensions, a strict definition of information in the digital context. From this point of view, human drawing articulates the animal and the machine. But it does so by objectifying the drawing, a process intimately linked with power. Neither machines nor animals undertake such an act. But the double nature of drawing, as anthropomorphic and zoomorphic, suggests that the power is a two-way flow: that the drawing subjects us as much as we objectify it. Human drawing of animals might then be characterised as the process of visualising the visible in such a way that it becomes a conduit for invisible relations between phyla. It remains to be seen whether that project is possible.

Consideration

As the phenomenological tradition has attested for a generation, to see is to be seen, to belong to the visible. If we appropriate the world to our desires, we are also appropriated. The question then is: what does the world desire? Drawing on the maverick biology of Caillois (1984) and Portmann (1967), Kaja Silverman argues that animals, insects, even stones appear in forms that cannot be explained by the usual scientific concepts (survival, camouflage, display). Rather, they exist to display themselves for perception in the visible world, perception therefore by humans, that unique species in which perception as aesthesis has become a speciality. 'What I am calling "appearance"', she writes, 'occurs only through the most paradoxical of all events: the meeting of absence and presence' (Silverman 2000: 144), a meeting which is ontological as much as semiotic. As a result of the abstraction of being, in the form of signs, from the living, breathing world, we humans 'only give the gift of Being to something when we permit it inaccurately to replicate what was' (Silverman 2000: 145): that is, to become a signifier not of the lost creature but of the specific and personal history of repression which originates the signifying activity of the individual.

There is a hint of arrogance in presuming that the world exists in order for us to (mis)understand it. Why should human perception be so privileged? Silverman's answer derives from the psychoanalytic tradition, and pertains to the unique formation of human desire in the emergence into Lacan's Symbolic domain, the region of psychic life ordered into meaning by social and semiotic structuring. Human desire is founded on loss and lack, while animal instinct is presumably ordered by presence and fullness, since it is never mediated by those prohibitions that shape humanity. May there be a consciousness other than human to whom the significance of the world is more deeply comprehensible than it is to our species? Silverman is right to emphasise that it is a duty to act as if we were the only sentient species in the universe. Unless we care, we the dominant species on our all-too limited planet, then there will be no beauty to exhaust us with its appearing. But to suggest that the world exists only to end in our perception seems to mark a dangerous political line, a permission to restructure the world in the image not of our best interests, nor in the interests of the ecology itself, but to correspond with our often tragic desires. By way of contrast, Stephen J Gould argues that it is only because homo sapiens (and the whole chordata phylum) is a product of contingency that 'We are the offspring of history, and must establish our own paths' (Gould 1989: 323). In the course of emphasising our insubstantiality and lack of essence, Silverman elides the significance of our accidence, our contingent materiality. The actuality of being human is dependent on the accumulated history of evolution and mutation, by definition a randomising process. It is the dialectic of determination by randomness that makes us those heirs of history that have the job of making it. This dialectic at once severs us from the animal world and demands that we constantly revisit and reunify with it.

Most of us would accept the proposition that the natural world is, by and large, beautiful. Some would go further. Gaston Bachelard, for example, proposes that 'A need to animalize . . . is at the origins of imagination. The first function of imagination is to create animal forms' (cited in Bleakley 2000: 40). One element of this imaging imagination is caught in Lacan's famous thesis of the mirror phase. This first visual recognition of the human shape is not only the beginning of self-consciousness; it depends upon the recognition of an animal form as coincident with the emergent psyche. Counter to Agamben and to Silverman, it is animals, inclusive of humans, who bring meaning to the world, not least because they are the first distinguishing element against which the meaning of psyche is defined. Speaking, knowing, reasoning all come later. What initiates the human is the first recognition of the animal. That inclusive exclusion is the first act of meaning, making possible all others.

At the same time, this 'first' moment is dependent on being meant, that is on the deference of the animal to becoming signified; but also on being meaning, that is on the agreement of the animal to becoming signifier. The external animal and the internal animal body of the infant alike must become both the objects of signification and the active material and energetic bearers of meaning, of difference, and of the mediation which alone makes communication and understanding real. This is the significance of Lippit's reference to children and photographs as alike 'media': human beings signify, but they do so on the same basis as animals: that any body in the world radiates meaning, communicates its presence, its movement, its scent.

Animals, including human animals, signify simply by living. The efflorescence of nature's aesthetic loveliness, or its sheer sensuousness of touch, taste, smell as well as sound and vision, may or may not be entirely given for human perception, and may or may not, as Alan Bleakley argues, so teach us a moral fable:

> It is the animals themselves who will surely lead us to reformulate the ecological crisis, as we respond to their intentions, for the animals already show that they do not want an an-aesthetic life, a life of numbing insensitivity, a half-life. Rather they will awaken us through their sensitivities, their aesthetic presence, to our self-imposed numbness to the world (Bleakley 2000: 37)

This aesthetic account of animal display is close to the thesis of animal drawing, but despite Bleakley's contention that birdsong is a generous excess which demonstrates that birds too relish free time, the mode of temporality of a bird's song is different to the dimensionality of human drawing. The song and its singer are inextricable. But the drawing (as later the recording) are extricable and routinely extricated from their environments. In fact the figure-ground relation defines an exclusively human mode of signifying through objectification. In drawing, the human mind lifts the animal, including especially its own a priori animality, into the domain of object, without which it cannot be subject, cannot be mind at all. By eliminating gesture, technological drawing eliminates the physical. The CGI animal, and its more advanced offspring a-life, is free of this burden of physicality. Alienated from the gross physical world, it is in the position which Silverman mooted of representation: it can depict the loss of animals and animality, by tracing their coming into being as in-significant, as lacking the dimensionality that confers object status. Neither animals nor the human body have, in the digital, any necessity to stand as objects. Knowledge of things passes into knowledge as array, as data, as statistics of performances and behaviours atomised and particulate, freed of the continuity that objects have in Kant's logic of dimensions. Nor do digital animals have the properties of bare living. But this doesn't eliminate brute life. On the contrary, it frees the living creature of the obligations of space and time, the obligation of Being. The CGI gods can die without dying because they are datasets. The green world can return better than before because Being, the presence-to-self which Heidegger mourned as passing away, is revealed as a function of technologisation, not its fading counterpart. Heidegger believed that technology stood between the world and human perception. But in technological drawing, perception of the drawn acts to liberate the living creature from the obligation to be. Being was always a function of the separation of processes (such as life) from their environments. Freed of that separation, the creature can return to its process, to its becoming, without, however, sacrificing Commoner's (1971: 33) first law of ecology: everything is connected to everything else.

What Commoner's 'law' suggests is that in some way, the drawing of animals is a connection with them. The drawing of a particular animal may be a homage and an embrace of that animal itself. In animated films, the drawn is more likely to be of a typical example, an essential lion cub, let's say. In both instances, if Commoner is correct, the act of drawing is not just a reaching out by men and women towards an or some animals, but reciprocally a way that animals stretch out their beings to us, at least their visibility, and in animations their movement, towards the people who draw them. As my dog Zebedee draws her territory in scent, she draws me in, as when I draw her I invite her. But she communicates to me in movements, behaviours, shapes she makes with her body that I can draw, and in moving and behaving as it were for me, she is a partner in the drawing.

'If a lion could talk', wrote Wittgenstein towards the end of the *Philosophical Investigations*, 'we could not understand him' (Wittgenstein 1968: 223). Here the philosopher extends his thesis of language games to argue that, if animals do communicate, they do so in ways that we cannot possible comprehend because we do not share the rules of their games. The thesis is taken up by Jean-François Lyotard (1985), who argues that language games are so incompatible with one another that no attempt to make them so can succeed, or should, since it would introduce a position from which a game of games, a metagame, comprehending them all, could claim legitimacy over all of them. But as Samuel Weber points out in his afterword to Lyotard's book, the claim that language games are mutually incomprehensible is itself a meta-statement, the domination of the prescriptive statement '*thou shalt not let one language game impinge upon the singularity of anothe*r' (Weber in Lyotard 1985 104). Lyotard's argument recalls Niklas Luhmann's (2000) systems-theoretic account of the mass media, which likewise argues that each social system is 'autopoetic': bounded, self-organising, and treating all other neighbouring systems as environmental inputs and no more. Weber's counterargument applies equally to Luhmann. Communicative systems broach one another precisely because they are communicative. Not only does one national media system bleed into its neighbours', as Luhmann acknowledges, but media leak into legal, economic, political and social systems to the extent that attempts to distinguish them appear as policing manoeuvres rather than statements about how things operate. In the same way, Cary Wolfe (2003) intimates, the distinction between animal and human communicative systems cannot be regulated by prescription (a term which in Wolfe carries self-contradictory echoes of Derrida's philosophy of writing).

Depicting animals is perpetually fraught, a constant testament to the difficulty of the simultaneous drawing together and drawing apart of the drawer and the drawn. Such learning from and experiencing with is often enough an act of restitution, as Berger suggested, for the elimination of animals from our daily lives and increasingly from our planet, a recognition at best, at worst a consolation for the guilt we bear for their disappearance. At the same time recognition and consolation should not necessarily be frowned upon. Where animals give themselves for vision, the communication is not entirely one sided. *Chicken Run*, whose chickens, rats and dogs are only remotely connected to their animal originals, and which, like the characters of *Animal Farm*, unashamedly enact a human story in the allegorical form of the animal fable, still invites us to consider and briefly to inhabit a kind of animal utopia. Because the alternative is the hell of battery farming, however playfully glossed in the parody of *The Great Escape*, the quasi-human idyll without humans points not just towards a (probably too delicate) politics of animal rights, but the possibility of a counter zoomorphism in the film's audiences.

The socialism of *Chicken Run*'s closing pastoral is a far cry from the dying gods of *Mononoke*. There the last of shamanic religion persists: animation in connection with animism. In a secular age there will be few who elect to walk the way of the shaman, undertake the terrible psychic voyages of dying and rebirth, of being devoured and vomited back up again. New Age lip service to old faiths rarely coincides with the patient subjection to a god or animal over years of learning that characterises the ancient priests. Lightning fixes, like psychotropic drugs, deliver the goods without the years of sacrifice. But even those are the province of a handful of would-be spiritual voyagers. *Mononoke* certainly evokes, and its evocation seems to have rung strongly in Japan, those old animistic beliefs, and yet the resolution it proposes has to exceed them. Like *The Lord of the Rings*, *Mononoke* concerns itself with the fading of the old gods and the necessity to build a new order in their absence. Reverence remains, of course, but forest and mine, leaf and iron, must organise a synthesis of their own on the graves of ancient divinity. Though history is far from over, it may be that we all live after Ragnarok, the last day of the Norse myths, and that the ancient world lies as bones beneath our feet. Yet the old gods have left a legacy that drives the new confederation: something less glamourous than shamanic rituals, but as demanding in a quieter way.

The Lady Eboshi, the Emperor's stooge and the warring gods alike take what they need and damn the consequences. These are the instigating moments of the narrative. What those who survive must learn is that the consequences are still there: that actions have reverberations. It is not that each from henceforth will give up action – far from it. But that each must take account of the others, and of debts and responsibilities owed to the world. I take from my mother a word for this: consideration. This modest virtue concerns alertness to others and to the world. A considered gesture is one that applies only the effort necessary – the opposite of clumsiness. Considering is also a timely virtue: it takes time, however little, to consider the effects of an action, on oneself and others. It is a virtue because it is an invitation to being human to the fullest, to open communication with the human and natural worlds now and in the future. To that extent democratic rather than individualist, consideration as proposed by *Princess Mononoke* proposes that understanding the richness of the world requires responding to it with grace and tact. These are the virtues of the world left by the gods at the end of the film, surely not an ethics without guilt, but also a kind of innocence.

4

The Blue Planet

Virtual Nature and Natural Virtue

SEA. Bottomless. Symbol of infinity. Inspires deep thoughts. At the seaside one should always have a telescope. When contemplating the sea, always exclaim 'Water, water everywhere!' Flaubert, *Dictionary of Received ideas* (1976: 325).

Innocence and Wonder

Growing up in a small market town in rural Lincolnshire among the exposed eastern flatlands of England, Saturday afternoons had a special aura. We Catholics would, at a certain age, be expected at confession, sometime between 2.00 and 4.00 o'clock. In the beeswax-scented church we would huddle in our balaclavas by the stained deal confessional, rehearsing the self-accusations that alone would guarantee that our innocence would be washed in the blood of the lamb, sanctioned by ritual, sacralised and sacrificed the following day when, queuing for communion, we would provide our elders with the spectacle of holy simplicity on which the artifice of faith depends.

But at just those hours, between 2.00 and 4.00 of a Saturday afternoon, the children's matinees would run at the Starlight Picturedrome between the church and the level crossing, a pebble-dashed building with some cheap stucco ornaments in the Deco style which now seem poor and jejune but then, and even today in certain evening lights, evoked the mystery and delight, the delirium of *Captain Video*, *The Phantom Empire, First Spaceship on Venus*, all the terrific zooming through galaxies and thundering through caverns that a small boy could inhabit in the 1950s.

So we would quietly elbow and nudge our way as close to the dread door of the confessional as decency and the long-confessing elderly ladies would allow, then slow just enough to recite to the hidden priest in tones that we believed betokened suitable respect the trivial tale of venial sins to the tobacco-stained soutane glimpsed through the raffia grill. The form of words once told, we could sprint to the nearest pew, hurl ourselves to bruised, short-trousered knees and hurtle through the rosary at speeds that would baffle a Pentium processor. The task of Our Fathers and Hail Marys rendered to the satisfaction of all the saints in heaven, we could tiptoe to the huge door with its circle of roped iron in place of a handle, hauling it open and dragging it shut with quiet respect for those whose faith we shared, before turning to the sudden light, free to fly like birds scattering shoppers and ducks, dodging cars and bicycles, to arrive glowing with sacramental cleanliness and perspiration at the glass box office window. On the screen unfolded adventures which, I now know, were already fifteen or more years old, coming from years before my birth, before my conception, before original sin. In the Picturedrome's enfolding dark I discovered that innocence which my Church had taught me to prize, but which it had stolen away in the moment that it named it.

For the rest of the week, in the playground and in our ink-stained exercise books, those pictures were re-enacted, and the space between Our Lady of Good Counsel RC Primary School's cheap late Victorian gothic and the twenties instrumentalist architecture of the Sharp's Seeds warehouse would ring with the catchphrases of our celluloid heroes. 'Shazam!' and you would run at full tilt, one fist extended in front of your face, one trailed behind in the imaginary wind; 'Ride like the wind!' and in the immemorial pantomime of a broken trot, one hand holding invisible reins, the other slapping your hip, you rode down the mesas of unknown California. When my father died and the adult world came with its puberty and jobs, the school film club was even more a haven, a still exhalation of that disappearing innocence. Now *Lord Jim* and Michael Caine enacted the rites of cinematic faith, the call of the screen always an invitation to an act of worship. A certain fullness of experience, a certain loss of care, an obliteration of the days: a religion. The experience of cinema was always of enchantment.

Even when, as an undergraduate, I spent long hours at the Arts Cinema with Makaveyev and Has, Godard and Fellini, Faraldo's *Themroc* and Kosintsev's *Lear*, the arty self-consciousness of student life never really damaged the absorption of self into the passing images. To me cinema has always been timeless. Even after thirty years of study, I love more than any others those films that promote, in however complex a way, the state of grace which I can no longer demand from a religion to which, however, I owe in all gratitude my guiltless lack of faith.

There are always two pasts that any narration of media history must address: the time of history and the time of biography. For each of us, as Paddy Scannell eloquently argues (Scannell 1996), the intensity of those early experiences will continue to guide our deeply personal involvement in media institutions. For me that first production of guileless innocence, forever bound in with the confessional construction of innocent guile, still guides me through the now less intimately welcoming foyers towards the catechism of the frame. Nowadays, when we saunter out no longer blinded by the afternoon sun to talk of shots and ideology, I recognise the sociological and technical constructions of innocence, not least the innocence of children. I only claim that I was and remain affected by that imaginary purity, perhaps more so than the regretful adults who watched us parade towards the

Eucharist on Sunday morning. I want to confess, as if back in the deal box in the Catholic nave, that I am still embraced by that innocence, which is not regressive but marginalised, which cinema at its most sublime can still evoke. In thrall to the most totalitarian of effects extravaganzas,if I were capable of speech, I would be able to shout out in the piping voice of my childhood, "I am innocent".

If I say that this innocence is not regressive, it is because it is strictly speaking timeless rather than nostalgic. Like the sacraments of childhood, it is a gateway to a world without time. I have been lucky. The contemporary cinema of North America is more and more devoted to just this achievement of innocence. Of course, to achieve purity in an age like ours, and to achieve it among haggard and jaded adults, is like a victory: it cannot be achieved without those atrocities, news of which is carefully kept from the monuments and celebrations. If Jean Baudrillard were right, I would say that what we have is the simulation of innocence, but that would not be true, because the effect of which I speak, while it is technologically achieved, is not itself technological but experiential and affective, and there is no unreality in the world of affects. This innocence of the movies is as real and as true as any innocence ever was, but that is not very much. Innocence was always an artifice, biographically and ideologically. It has a history, especially in the 19th century Romantic cult of childhood (on whose 'impossibility' see Rose 1984). Indeed, it is in that cult that we find the first descriptions of the the technical device used to achieve that filmic state of grace: the sublime.

Beauty is ephemeral: by its nature it cloaks what changes: a lover, a landscape, a work of art. Beauty is our highest expression of what it is to be mortal. But innocence and the sublime transcend this terminal horizon to speak to us not of the afterlife but of a life unbounded by the horizon of death, and perhaps without the stain of birth: a timeless time of the infinite. In my green youth, it was the fabulous world of outer space that called to me through the glittering screen. Today it is as likely to be the spectacle of the ocean, which from the earliest films of the Lumières showed its intense affinity with the cinema. Perpetually changing, forever the same, light moving on water is, like cinema, a contradictory delight and, unlike anything else we watch on screen, never resolutely lost in time. Natural history documentary, and the documentary as an element in fiction, comes closest to absolute spectacle in the image of Ocean, and it is there that beauty and the sublime meet in a moment of innocence. This sublime and innocent effect, incongruously and unconsciously evoked in Lyotard's essay on 'Acinema' in the figure of the child playing with matches (Lyotard 1978), belong to a different order of time from narration, dependent on time's passing and its loss. Mesmerising, it is the time of the fetish.

Perhaps it is unnecessary to rehearse the Freudian theory of the fetish: the deliberate construction of a psyche innocent of sexual difference through the displacement of anxiety attached to the sight of genital difference onto some accidentally proximate object (Freud 1977). I do not claim that waves and water are necessarily sexual: on the contrary – they may obtain their energy from displaced sexual anxiety, but the recirculation of that energy is as specifically asexual as it is immortal. Sexuality, like mortality, is a temporal phenomenon, structured by the yes and the no. Always negotiated, it has its narratives, its direction through time, its goals and its regrets. But the sublime knows nothing of that, denies and annihilates it in the vast emptiness of obscene completion. The sublime, it must be said, is a property of the mind, not of the world: it is a surrender to the otherness of the world, and even more to an invisible abstraction of worldness or of deity that exceeds not only human comprehension – and therefore communication – but the world itself. In this philosophical definition, the sublime is quite distinct from the cinema of special effects. Such effects lie athwart the linear dimensions of narrative, providing the monotony of story with a release into another vector; and on occasion the spectacle of the film has ambitions to exceed the dimensions of the cinematic, the medium demonstrating its own power to exceed mediation itself. On those occasions, cinema communicates not the sublime – which is by definition incommunicable – but the idea of sublimity. In such films death serves the function of terminal communication, what cannot be spoken. This cinematic sublime constructs an apparatus for the imitation of that zero degree of speech, and so constructs, as an object of awe, an event that contradicts its own existence. But there is another mode of apprehension that permits a shock of non-recognition, and yet refuses the blandishments of a pseudo-religious surrender to the absolute. The phenomenologist Maurice Merleau-Ponty refers to it as '*being filled with wonder*', explaining 'that in order to see the world and grasp it as paradoxical, we must break with our familiar acceptance of it and, also, from the fact that from this break we can learn nothing but the unmotivated upsurge of the world' (Merleau-Ponty 1962: xv). The phenomenological method of bracketing off our familiar, socialised representations and expectations in order to see the world with fresh eyes is distinguished from the sublime in two ways. Firstly, it proposes that once the blinkers of habit are removed, the world can and indeed must be perceived, because humans and their world are of one stuff. And secondly, it suggests that the world, and implicitly human apprehension of it, is without ulterior or external force, lacking in goals or motives, and instead can be experienced as a constant welling up into existence. This sense of wonder is not only communicable: it is of its nature a communication, based on removing the blockages that otherwise prevent the world from experiencing humans, as much as humans experiencing nature. Against the sublime's pretence of a timeless, universal and to that extent unnatural order bordering and potentially overmastering our own, although forever alien to it, wonder poses laying bare the flesh, the eyes, the nose and ears to experience the world anew. That, initially, is the meaning of innocence.

Watching Waves

Black browed albatross flying over crashing waves {Diomedea melanophrys} Falklands Is. Production still from *The Blue Planet*. Photograph © Ben Osborne/ naturepl.com

It is this innocence that in the first instance, shapes the television persona of David Attenborough: schoolboy enthusiasm in a seventy-year-old man. Perhaps uniquely among senior television personalities, Attenborough seems universally popular, the best director general the BBC never had. In a career spanning decades, including running BBC2, introducing colour to British screens, and fathering the blockbuster TV documentary (including *Civilisation* and *The Ascent of Man* as well as his own *Life On Earth*), Attenborough has collected nothing but accolades (see Cubitt 1997). His personality as much as his voiceover dominates the reception of *The Blue Planet*, 2002's eight-part 'natural history of the oceans', just as his presence on screen must have helped Discovery Channel make their investment in an extremely expensive series. The surprise success of television series on sell-through DVD must have been a bonus, but the BBC's unusual license-fee funding structure is very probably responsible for the existence of the series at all: very few large-scale documentaries, and those usually with far clearer human interest angles, get made in purely commercial television circles. Even so, the series required a partner, both financially and politically. The BBC's license fee is voted on by the British parliament, and the corporation's balance between ratings success and public interest programming is under constant scrutiny from left and right. Partnerships with overseas companies guarantee not only a pre-sale but presence in the crowded international markets for television programming where most television series will find their eventual profits. As much as the networks of scientists, conservationists and researchers involved in production, this infrastructure of distribution is critical to the very existence of series of this order, a genre which the BBC has very nearly made synonymous with itself. The structures of international broadcasting, what Peter Watkins (2001) calls the universal clock, is clearly visible in the episodic structure, where individual stories never extend over the 12 minute mark, at which the standard four minute advertising break is usually placed. Though the BBC does not carry advertising, many of the broadcasters it sells on to do, and their revenue stream has to take precedence over the aesthetics and even the science of *The Blue Planet* (we will see an example of a different episodic structure in Chapter 6). These distributive structures underlie and shape the series and its delivery to audiences. To a great extent, the success of TV material on DVD must be attributable to the desire to watch through without the interruption of commercial breaks, so much so that ordinary viewers will part with substantial sums for box sets (not just academics who can recoup the cost in tax, research budgets and kudos).

Equally significant is the distribution of knowledge through this exercise in the popular communication of science. The programme must equilibrate the public service ethos of informing and educating with the requirements of entertainment. In order to acquire sales, hold audiences and build a viable vehicle for promoting both scientific knowledge and broadly ecological themes, the series foregrounds its spectacular cinematography, marked by technical expertise, grandeur and rarity. Scale is important: the series opens with a sequence on blue whales. Rarity, like the bizarre brine lake of episode 2, and the sense of epic sweep secured in time-lapse sequences likewise feed into spectacle. In addition, the series topic has a special place in the history of cinematography. Since the Lumières first photographed boys diving into the sea, audiences have delighted in the play of light moving on water (Coe 1981: 71; Slide 1982: 65, 67). With the same meditative absorption with which we gaze onto the sea itself, we gaze into its picture on screen, the two processes bound by the abstraction they bring to viewers, the infantile pleasure in the sheer movement of light. It was just such absorbed distraction that early censure of cinema singled out for blame (Crary 1999), and that maritime science cannot but evoke, but which it must subsume into focused attention.

At another level, the experience of watching waves, or the strange and to that extent magical world of the sea, belongs with Benjamin's observation that 'nature is Messianic by reason of its eternal and total passing away' (Benjamin 1979:156). If Adorno was right in locating this as an early draft of the *Theses on the Philosophy of History*, then the sense of the Messiah here evoked is that eternally-present moment in history at which the Messiah might arrive, and which therefore sanctifies the present instant with the possibility that in it all history might be at once fulfilled and ended, 'time filled by the presence of the now', a 'leap in the open air of history', 'enough to blast open the continuum of history' (Benjamin 1969: 261-2) and, for Benjamin, therefore also fundamentally revolutionary. I cannot claim that being mesmerised by the ebb and flow of light on a TV screen is in some way a radical political action; but there is undoubtedly a utopian quality to it, a surrender to pleasure, to the infinite, and to infinite change, that provides not only respite from labour and a chance to recuperate, but a distant whiff of another life, unconstrained by the endless round of work and attention. Unlike Messianic time, the ocean's restlessness is a perpetual disappearance, a model for the disappearance of history (or in Marx's terms prehistory) in the emergence of the realm of freedom. This distant utopian gleam is reprised in the freedom of fish and birds, and perhaps most of all in their streamlined shapes, the perfection of their adaptation to their environments, and their ability to move in three dimensions. Like God's winged angels, these finned and feathered creatures appear as messengers of another and better mode of being.

This innocent utopia of the wild seas has a particular temporality. We consider recordings to be records of the past, but the experience of watching water is of a now that extends indefinitely. The precise configuration of light in the frames that pass by is irreplaceable, but another, infinitely or infinitesimally different, will always supersede it, so that its timelessness is not that of the philosophical absolute but of an endlessly differentiating repetition. I believe this is what allows the image of light on water to approximate to Charles Sanders Peirce's description of 'Firstness', 'Feeling, the consciousness which can be included with an instant of time, passive consciousness of quality without recognition or analysis' (Peirce 1991: 185). In Peirce's scheme, firstness names the perception of a phenomenon before its source is separated out as an object ('secondness') and named ('thirdness'). This moment of pure perception without objectivisation or significance can be, as it is here, intensely pleasurable. In this context, it suggests, the sea is intrinsically valuable because it is beautiful. A utopia notably lacking in human beings or warnings about pollution – that task is reserved for the tail-gunning documentary 'Deep Trouble' presented by series director Martha Holmes, who does an excellent job of arguing for the unequal distribution of blame, with the fads of the wealthy the most dangerous to aquatic life. But such is not Attenborough's line. There is little mention of rarity and none of endangered status. This utopianism depends instead on recognising the elegance of the whole system as well as its mysteries, in short the beauty of the seas. Distinctions between one environment and another in the episode titles ('Tidal Seas', 'Coral Seas' and so forth) scarcely impinge on the message of the introductory episode: that all of these ecosystems interact between themselves and with the terrestrial and meteorological environments to boot. Only missing is the human, except for the familiar screen presence and insightful science of Attenborough himself, whose sheer seniority if nothing else allows him to speak, not for the oceans which are presumed to speak for themselves, but for the scientific community that seeks to understand them.

The Blue Planet, as Robert Frost had it of poetry, begins in delight and ends in wisdom, but is that wisdom, deprived of political analysis, merely a beatifically meditative state? Or is it the necessary Temporary Autonomous Zone which we need, argues Hakim Bey, because without some experience of liberation, the struggle to achieve it would be abstract and empty? A case can certainly be made that *The Blue Planet* is a work of art, where art is a work of delight and wisdom which attains a certain autonomy from human or indeed any other interests. In this sense it is no criticism to say that the series lacks ethics: unlike ethics, aesthetics is not bound to answer the question 'for whom?'. Similarly science, where it is a disinterested pursuit of knowledge, can seek knowledge for its own sake as art can aspire to art for art's sake. Yet it is also the case that the beautiful, contra some environmentalist thinkers (Leopold 2001 for example), is beautiful to the extent that it can be discussed. The old adage '*de gustibus non est disputandum*' holds good only because it is impossible to persuade people to change their idiosyncratic tastes: every taste can be argued. Only the sublime is beyond discussion. Beauty and ugliness exist along a continuum. Where we place a particular species on that continuum is a matter of taste. What these programmes raise is the system's beauty rather than that of its individual denizens, and the quality singled out for marvel is the creativity of the system: not just what it has produced, but the power of invention that slots life into every available and many apparently unavailable niches. Marvelling at the ecosystem, enjoying the beauty or ugliness of its denizens, these are on the one hand sheerly scientific pleasures, but they are also, where marine biology is prepared to make its case, the elements of wonder as a secular virtue, a delight in the water because it is lovely, and in its inhabitants as something more than dinner.

Truth and Style

It is always possible to raise the Madagascar periwinkle argument for preserving biodiversity. That small plant yields vincristine and vinblastene, widely used in the treatment of leukaemia. It gives its name to the argument that we never know which unassuming scrap of life might yield some vital service to humanity. But it is not an argument raised in the series whose ultimate beneficiaries are not, or not exclusively human. This beauty is presented, it may well be, as grounds for a subsequent persuasion, which could stretch from recommending a career in marine biology to a commitment to veganism. Its celebration of creativity is, however, also systemic, neither individuated by species nor personalised as the property of a single fish or mollusc. Creativity inheres in a system which both promotes creativity and evolves through the creative processes it enables and nurtures. Both considered and considerate, *The Blue Planet* exhibits a kind of structured respect for that subjectless creativity, without requiring that it be like, in some sense yet to be fathomed, the life of the mind or like art. Without the anthropomorphisms that create the comedy in Besson's *Atlantis*, like Besson's film *The Blue Planet* rejoices in sheer movement. But Attenborough clearly enjoys not only the obviously aesthetic moments – a dolphin pod leaping into the sun – but also the scientific first and the technically challenging; deep sea mitochondria or the nocturnal ejaculations of a coral reef. Given the complexity of any ecosystem, and the near impossibility therefore of photographing it qua system, such moments stand metonymically for the principle that 'everything connects with everything else' (Commoner 1971: 33).

The theme of nature's endless creativity and the mesmerising firstness of the waves should not, however, diminish the sense that nature too has a history. If, in a phrase Stephen Jay Gould attributes to Dave Ramp, "To a first approximation, all species are extinct' (Gould 1989: 216), absolute conservation is not an option, indeed Edward O. Wilson estimates the extinction rate of species at about one species per million per year (Wilson 2002: 99). Change is the rule, not the absolute homeostasis of the perpetually self-identical which Hegel derided as the night in which all cows are black (Hegel 1977: 9). Commenting on the mystical Oneness ascribed to nature by new age ecologists in the light of this adage, Murray Bookchin argues that humanity's separation from nature, far from unique, is typical of evolutionary history:

> We must see that *every* process is also a form of alienation, in the sense that differentiation involves separation from older forms of being as well as the absorption of what is negated into the new, such that the whole is the richly varied fulfilment of its latent potentialities (Bookchin 1996: 76)

Bookchin's idiosyncratic reading of natural creativity – a belief that life-forms are self-directed and participate in their own evolution – embraces the Hegelian process of subsumption (*Aufhebung*) in which time is the dialectical process of overcoming and assimilating oppositions. Explicitly rejecting negative readings of Hegel, Bookchin wants to regard evolution as a process of increasing complexity and order driven through moments of differentiation and its overcoming. Unlike the poststructural theory of difference, Bookchin reads difference as a positively productive process. To make an analogy, the structural analysis of images isolates the vanishing point as the origin of perspective in painting and cinematography; Bookchin's philosophy would read the same point as the alienating moment of differentiation from which the ordered complexity of the image evolves. Rather than a gap or lack, for Bookchin differentiation is a process of emergence and branching paths of opportunity and development. It is in this sense that the firstness I have tried to identify in *The Blue Planet* might be understood: as a principle of perpetual flowering, a welling out of unnamed and as yet unrealised potentialities, rather than as a record of disappearance. Likewise the sense of the present tense of these images derives not from a timeless nature apart from human understanding but from the meaning of the present as that unique moment in which the future is perpetually springing into existence. And finally, this is the logic of the theme of ignorance that runs through the series – ignorance of the vastest ecosystem on the planet. At any moment, and at several during the shooting of the series, new phenomena and new species are emerging into the light of knowledge, and the future contains millions of unknown species. This articulation of science not as a body of knowledge but as a process of discovery is key to the portrayal of science as joyful, synthesising the BBC's remit, to inform, educate and entertain.

Yet the very virtuosity of the series' production raises a curious dilemma. To define a pristine nature, to communicate its privilege over the ordinarily political, and to place it in a public realm where its virtues can be implicitly contrasted with the viciousness of the forces that endanger it, the series uses high end technologies. In Episode 2, devoted to 'The Deep', Attenborough's commentary emphasises the absence of light at depths below 800 metres, demonstrated in one sequence by turning off the headlights of the camera submersible to observe bioluminescence, and in another with reference to the especially strong filtering out of red light, demonstrating the camouflage benefits of deep red colouring, and the predatory power of illuminating and seeing in the red end of the spectrum. Both sequences demand complex lighting and grading to allow viewers to see both the emitted light and the outlines of the creatures that make them. A female angler fish, whose bright lure is featured in one of *Finding Nemo*'s more memorable sequences, must be lit only parsimoniously if the relative brightness of the lure is to be apparent. While some of this can be achieved in camera, more must be the result of pushing different areas of the image during the digital grading process in post-production.

Nature as special effect – Female Anglerfish - Deep sea species from Atlantic Ocean {Caulophryne sp.}. Production still from *The Blue Planet*. Photograph © David Shale / naturepl.com

Meanwhile, given that we are told that only five submersibles are capable of reaching the depths navigated by Alvin, we are treated to a shot of Alvin descending into a deep trench below the abyssal plain. Whether this is shot from a second, invisible and uncommented submersible, a reconstruction at shallower depth or a digital effect or composite, it is deeply evocative of the intense technologisation required to secure pictures from 'The Deep' oceans. Scientific realism is often a matter of readjusting the unobservable so that it can be observed. The human eye cannot see in the majority of the electromagnetic spectrum: instruments observe on our behalf, and false-colour algorithms allow us to see the phenomena they gather reduced to the red, green and blue that we can perceive. And if, as becomes apparent from the accompanying 'Making Waves' documentary, the whale carcass so darkly populated by hagfish was towed and sunk so that they could be filmed, surely this has the validity of scientific experimentation, if it brings the bonus of filmed footage of a previously unfilmed sleeper shark? The unaided human cannot swim much below ten or twenty metres. Whatever there is to discover of nature, as knowledge or beauty, will have to be gathered with the aid of technology.

The relation is reciprocal. The newer digital technologies seem to draw inspiration from these weirdly glittering deep sea jellies, so evocative of the spinning spacecraft of Spielberg's *Close Encounters*, not to mention the angler fish in *Nemo*. Attenborough's commentary singles out 'another twilight monster, Phonyma, the inspiration for the *Alien* movies', a conscious evocation of the special effects of blockbuster cinema to counterbalance the spectacle of such unexpected species. The soundtrack meanwhile evokes nothing so much as Louis and Bebe Barron's score for *Forbidden Planet*, entirely electronic. Though the series uses dolphin clicks and whale song as occasional accompaniments, for the most part the sounds of underwater species are not strongly signalled. In 'The Deep', the challenge is the greater since, presumably, the immense water pressure would allow only subsonics, and large numbers of the species shown are soft-bodied and would make little if any noise.

Television, perhaps because of its origins in radio, is unfriendly towards silence, perhaps even more so than cinema, where music may have been introduced to drown out the chatter of the projector and the hiss of the old arc lamps. Nor is the sound of the submersible's motors, of aqualungs and the technical chat of the scientists and camera operators sufficient to accompany the images. Yet in other episodes, George Fenton's score is for the most part orchestral in tone, and the sound effects most commonly of water itself, with occasional great swishes and swooshings for the passage of shoals. For the section of episode three devoted to comb jellies' nightly forays to the near-surface waters in search of inchling fish spawn, some of the same electronic themes re-emerge, but now accompanied by a melodic use of long, complex chords. Elsewhere in the same episode, an ornamental but fearsome swimming crab is introduced with music from the Peking Opera. But in 'The Deep', the sounds associated with the most alien species, the jellies and arthropods, evoke extraterrestrial scenarios, with more recognisable sounds like electric guitar reserved for relatively comprehensible if still bizarre predators like the fangtooth and the hairy angler, for whose hunting, however, Fenton also deploys, humorously, stock musical phrases – tiptoes in the dark, menace of the haunted house. Calling up memories of the genres most associated with special effects – science fiction and horror – sets up a zonal boundary between 'The Deep's and the shallows, a transition vividly caught in the move from distant electronic cries and reverberations to a lilting four-note theme accompanying the journey of firefly squid toward the surface in a sequence which ends with a majestic brass fanfare as the sun rises, The closer the series approaches to the familiar world of air, the more natural its sounds become, both in instrumentation and in direct sound recording of birds and marine mammals. The further it strays into domains where humans can only survive protected by advanced technologies, the stranger both sounds and musical elements become.

The editing too rejoices at significant moments in its artifice. Many of the sequences are necessarily brief, given the circumstances of finding and recording creatures in the vast expanses of the open sea. Some sequences are compiled to communicate a topic, such as the understated crossfades between miscellaneous grazers and predators heading for shallow waters in what is described as a convoy in the voice-over. At precisely this moment, a downward pan across the body of a predator is used as a wipe to reveal a shoal of squid rising to the surface. Elsewhere the rising moon serves the same purpose. A more telling example comes in the fade in 'The Deep' episode introducing the descent to the abyssal plain. Viewed in slow-motion, the scale of the ocean floor changes, from the backdrop to a tiny CGI submersible to a close-up inspection of its component sand and rock. Given the cloudiness and darkness of underwater shooting, photography alone is incapable of conveying the three-dimensional scale of the undersea environment, and the programme makers have to use some form of artifice. Graphs, maps, even Earth-observation satellite images are all more obviously mediated constructions. The decision to go with CGI would then appear to be grounded in a desire for immediacy, a paradox in that immediacy as affect can only be achieved through the most highly mediated technologies. As Bazin observed half a century ago, 'realism in art can only be achieved one way – through artifice' (Bazin 1971: 26). The hallmark techniques of Bazinian realism – the long take and especially deep focus – require advanced technological devices and technical skills. At a certain point, Bazin admits, pursued for its own sake the artifice takes over from the mission to reveal reality. *The*

Blue Planet, at moments like these, hovers on that borderline, not so much because of an intoxication with the possibilities of the medium as because the vocation towards communicating marine biology and the ordinary techniques of scientific observation meet in indirect observation and the trope of analogy that is so frequently deployed in the voice-over, in the score, and now in the communication of unphotographable scale.

Analogy is not fiction but rhetoric. For the opening sequence exploring the wreck of the *Titanic*, James Cameron secured the services of two of the five deep-sea capable submersibles, the Russian *Mir-1* and *Mir-2*. The remote-operated vehicle (ROV) Snoop Dog belongs to the *Mirs*, and the footage gathered aboard the wreck comes from dives made, with Cameron aboard, in September of 1995. Reverse angles of the ROV are model shots: even though both *Mirs* possessed one, the danger of placing two in enclosed spaces was too great. Similarly, shots of one or other submersible in proximity to the ship are location footage, but wide angles containing both are model shots, also required because Cameron's dives coincided with Hurricane Luis, which along with the rest of the season's hurricanes had stirred up even the silt on 'The Deep' sea bed. To recognise the fineness of the distinction, it is worth recalling that Cameron planned his dives using the same model that would be used in the effects shots, and that the model in turn derived from extensive video footage of the wreck secured during earlier dives. According to Paula Parisi, 'Dive time was so precious Cameron would often make the split-second decision to shoot the rehearsal move, putting him in the unusual position of shooting film the first time he laid eyes on something – the realm of the documentarian, not the feature filmmaker' (Parisi 1988: 67). Despite the intercutting of these shots with narrative dialogue scenes, there is a claim to be made that the model shots are true analogies of the location shots. But the analogies operate to tie the wreck to the fictional narrative that they introduce, the love triangle of Rose, Cal and Jack, adding to the ship's fictive geometry of gender and class the dimension of time, loss and healing. In *Titanic*, the rhetorical trope functions in relation to fiction.

In the BBC series, however, it works in relation to the popular communication of science. The analogical structure of the 'convoy' of deep sea denizens towards the night-time surface is conducted through montage, the individual creatures standing for a mass migration across the oceans by definition impossible to capture except *pars pro toto*. Indeed the whole series operates on a montage aesthetic, collecting details, no one of which contains the whole, until they add up to more than the sum of their parts. The anomaly of the CGI shots, however, is that they represent one of the rare instances in which human activity figures in the series, other than in the generic 'science', 'scientists', or 'we', denoting the human species. Thus where the Cameron sequence serves to humanise a deep sea phenomenon – the rattails winding through a sunken bedroom, for example – the CGI shot of the submersible in 'The Deep' episode serves to dehumanise and alienate the abyss. To return to Bookchin's argument about the necessary function of alienation, of making other, in the dialectic of evolution, the purpose of the shot, and particularly the shot transition is to establish the gulf that divides human and natural, but in order to pose the otherness of the natural as that which must be overcome in a new knowledge of nature which will renew the nature of knowledge.

Marine Ethics

This dialectical vision, while it may or may not be good science, opens a gateway through the aporias of environmental ethics. Among the contributors to Pojman's important anthology on the subject, Holmes Rolston III analyses four possible structures in which nature comes to have value. Anthropocentric ethics are grounded in human self-interest. Anthropogenic ethics stress human interest (without the 'self'), the value placed by humans on non-human life, exemplified by political or financial contributions to preserving Antarctica, a place few of us will ever visit for ourselves, but which most of us believe should remain untouched wilderness. Non-anthropogenic ethics stress the similarities between human and non-human, values shared across sentient species like a wolf's care for her cubs. The strongest ecological claim is for the intrinsic value of nature, a value not grounded in consciousness, as for example the way a plant values sunlight. In many respects, *The Blue Planet* embraces this last option. Its paeans to the sulphide and hydroxide-loving ecologies of the ocean floor, for example, suggest that the miracle of their existence is of value in and of itself. But in addition, the programme alerts viewers to the possibility of other undiscovered phyla lurking in the unexplored nine-tenths of the ocean deeps, suggesting that knowledge too is a virtue, and that knowledge of the natural world is likewise a good, regardless of its potential service to humans. The ethical dialectic is then between the unknown ecosystem which is a good in itself regardless of our knowledge, and knowledge which is also a good, regardless of its instrumental uses for human self-interest. The little CGI submersible then articulates a complex negotiation between alien and self, the unknown and knowledge. A virtual token of the tiny proportion of the sea that has been explored, it also signals the vast and precious mysteries that surround us, and the tact and caution required in exploring further.

Scientific realism is not the same as photographic realism, though photography is one of its instruments. Biologists are if anything more likely than physicists or chemists to embrace the elegance of systems rather than the potency of objects. As J Baird Callicott observes, here agreeing with Rolston, 'The ontological primacy of objects and the ontological subordination of relationships characteristic of a classical

Western science is, in fact, reversed in ecology' (Callicott 2001: 131). The challenges this raises for television are considerable, and the montage aesthetic adopted by *The Blue Planet* is remarkably good at overcoming it. At the same time, in order to capture and hold viewers long enough for such complex conceptualisations to be communicated, the show must attract visually and aurally. Here the dialectical vision Bookchin brings to bear is again useful. An aesthetic based exclusively on the intrinsic value of the natural world would have to portray it as innocent – innocent of human interests and human knowledge. An anthropocentric aesthetic would have to argue the case for the instrumental value of knowledge, in the development of new exploratory technologies and new pharmaceuticals or feed stocks.

But the series' negotiation between intrinsic and anthropogenic values avoids, for the most part, the sublime, unquestionable and unarguable, in favour of wonder and the beautiful. Its portrayal of nature is of an innocent world, a world of intrinsic values like food and reproduction, whose beauty arises from its interconnected and systemic order. But it is beautiful rather than sublime to the extent that nature arises as knowledge and therefore as something which is also simultaneously deeply, indeed intrinsically human. Montage, including composite cinematographic and CGI images, can only produce a virtual image of the unimaginably complex and vast processes of the oceans. Yet this virtual nature is a remarkable solution to the question of natural virtue. Imaging technologies capable of transcending their human origins allow the natural to remake what it is to be human. Human, natural and technological are three moments of a single process, for if we cannot know, we cannot care, and if we cannot recognise nature as at once ecologically bound to our own survival as a species and as an utterly distinct and to a great extent unknown category of existence, there can be no way of mediating the needs of these two torn halves of an integral world.

The gulf that opens up before us when we try to contemplate the natural world is not an artefact of the European Enlightenment as such. If anything the obverse is the case: scientific rationalism is a response to the *fait accompli* of nature's estrangement. Perhaps indeed for the feudal peasantry and the learned doctors who extrapolated from their practical knowledge, or for other peoples equally bound to the land, some closer implication in natural process was the norm. We must envy and learn from them all we can – but we cannot return to their estate. Still less can the globalising humanity of the 21st century, these teeming billions, acquaint themselves with the ocean, the very emblem of untamed and unexplored wilderness. As we will see in the next chapter, ignorance of the oceans has become a signal political failure. Knowledge of them is therefore vital. But there are few who understand the waters, and none who know the depths of the sea, so inimical to our species. There is little choice but to treat 'The Deep' as a world apart. In that sense, the abyssal ocean gives us a model of scientific exploration, an exploration whose end is wonder and the startling paradox of a world so intimately bound into our own and yet so unutterably strange.

More than that, however, is the lesson to be learned from how that exploration is undertaken, by which instruments, under what conditions, shaped by which discourses. On the one hand, we must first, with Merleau-Ponty, throw off expectations in order to see at all the remarkable variety and complexity of oceanic ecosystems; and with Peirce rejoice in the first sensuous embrace of the world. But if there is to be a relation, then we must also allow Bookchin's argument: the estrangement between humans and deep ocean has to be accepted and embraced too, because without it there can be no relation. That that relation is technological of necessity is of the essence: techne proves itself again the mediator, not only in the form of Gandalf's magic, but in the domain of the popular communication of science on TV. Writing some years ago the late Alex Wilson noted that

> Usually animals are the observed. The fact that they can observe us as well has lost all significance in everyday life . . . But on video and film we can make them return our look (something Disney is famous for) as if they could speak to us. Thus in some contemporary explorations of nature, it is not so much yet another frontier that is charted and explored as it is the memory of an archaic habitat – a time and place where we could communicate with animals (Wilson 1991: 152)

In *The Blue Planet* however it is neither the archaic habitat of *Princess Mononoke* nor the unreturnable, subjectless gaze of Berger and Lippit, but the necessity of inventing a mode of looking that encourages the world's unmotivated upsurge to well up into us, clasp itself to us, merge with the salt water in our veins. At last the reluctance of the series to prize the individual or even the species above the ecosystem as a whole becomes plain: the ocean as a whole looks back, feels us as surely as we feel it. The construction of technology as the pariah that embodies all the most evil elements of the polis and turns them against nature is not an alternative politics: it is the same politics as that which enslaves technology as well as nature and turns both to the purposes of greed and power beyond all pleasure – sure signs, right enough, of the old alpha male enacting his purely and merely natural functions beyond the bounds of reason. What the amazing, awesome, marvellous, wonderful sights and sounds of *The Blue Planet* indicates throughout is that techne is the only route through which we now can sense the world, most especially that part of the world's conversations which are not conducted in wavelengths we can hear, see or otherwise apprehend.

It is only in the age of scientific apparatuses, including movie and video cameras and microphones, that systems theory has been thinkable for humans. The formalisation of early biologists' intuition of an interwoven elaboration of life had to wait for statistical scientists working on telephone exchange design at Bell Labs. As massively parallel computing borrows from neuroscience, so too does biology borrow from communications concepts and techniques that have become central to the elaboration of an ethics worthy of the sea. If the core of such ethics is wonder, its corollaries are connectivity on the one hand – the imbrication of the human in the stories of the sea – and on the other the sheer autonomy of this complex environment. The intrinsic value thesis proposes axiomatically that nature has rights. To recognise the rights of nature is to recognise concomitantly its obligations. The question then is one of responsibility. What this analysis of *The Blue Planet* suggests is that there are at least two partners who bear responsibility for the larger ecosystem, three if we include the technological mediations between human and natural as equal partner in the construction of knowledge and care. To a great extent it can be argued that nature supplies its part of the bargain autonomously, digesting waste, producing natural capital. Yet if nature has natural virtue, and therefore obligations, according to traditional moral philosophy, it must also have the ability to refuse its obligations. Which brings us to the question of freedom.

Nature and Destiny

The Perfect Storm and Whale Rider

so few
have the polis
in their eye
Charles Olson, *Maximus Poems,* Letter 6, 2

Give Me Liberty Or . . .

Freedom is a tainted word. It has been rolled so often round the mouths of politicians that you no longer want to feel it in your own. And yet, for all the hypocritical saliva that sticks to it, freedom returns, and with a vengeance, as a fundamental question in the study of ecological media. Against the fragility of the biosphere and of any individual life, the immense forces of nature, from asteroids to earthquakes, present a spectacle of awe and terror. Either it will be possible to survive such forces and events or it will not. If it is not, then we must face our own annihilation or that of our children or our grandchildren or their children, and very possibly of the entire lifeworld. On the other hand, the available definitions of freedom are chilling in their implications. For Hegel, in the bowels of the dialectic, freedom and nothingness are synonymous: 'The supreme form of Nought as a separate principle would be Freedom; but Freedom is negativity in that stage, when it sinks self-absorbed to supreme intensity, and is itself an affirmation, and even absolute affirmation' (Hegel 1975: 128). Freedom, at this moment in Hegel's logic, is the negativity of negation, the readiness of all processes to abolish their predecessors, overcome and subsume them. Such a force cannot stop at overwhelming its opposite however: it must even negate itself, in an abyssal inward spiral of self-annihilation. It is this absolute destruction which, dialectically, returns as its obverse, the endlessly affirmative upwelling of the new. But however positively one tries to spin the negativity of freedom, this essence of freedom is unmistakably the most intense form of nothingness, an-nihilation, the very opposite of being. Freedom and destruction are one and the same.

A hundred and fifty years or so after Hegel, we find a similarly disturbing conception of Freedom in Jean-Luc Nancy: 'freedom', he argues, 'if it is something, is the very thing that prevents itself from being founded' (Nancy 1993: 12), and he goes on to propose that 'the freedom of being' as a philosophical category, is 'the infinite inessentiality of its being-finite, which delivers it to the singularity wherein it is "itself"' (1993: 14). Turning Hegel back on himself, Nancy asks what freedom might be if it were something (rather than the Hegelian nothing). It would, in the first instance, have no essence, since an essence is a necessary property, and freedom cannot be restricted by necessity. Freedom cannot be itself at all because, being free, it cannot be identical with anything. Only this lack of essence allows freedom to exist, but in an existence that has no being, in the strict sense of the word, since being entails, among other things, a self-identity which freedom, lacking essence, cannot have. For Hegel, freedom is the abstract motor of process, the negation and affirmation that drives change. Like the laws of physics, it is a constant in the dialectic. But for Nancy, freedom cannot, by definition, be either a law or a constant. Because it cannot be self-identical, freedom must always be other than itself. The ocean waves of *The Blue Planet* might stand then as the emblem Nancy's freedom. For Hegel, freedom is a moment of action; for Nancy it is the infinity of restless non-identity. Hegel's freedom is integral to the unfolding of the universe's self-appreciation as absolute: it belongs to time as the dimension of ineluctable progress towards a goal, the self-realisation of the absolute. Nancy's freedom has no goal, for that would constrain its freedom. Instead, it is the principle of a perpetually unstill flickering into and out of existence, goalless, timeless; a condition rather than a direction. If Hegel is right, we can expect nature to abide by a global ethical obligation, even though the full working out of its integration into the final moment of the absolute may have to wait until all of the dialectical processes are worked through. But if Nancy is correct, and there is neither goal nor direction to natural processes, then natural processes are beyond morality.

Both philosophers speak of the relationship between freedom and necessity, freedom and destiny. And it is to destiny we turn in this chapter as a first step towards an understanding, not of nature's founding principles, but of the ways in which it has been envisaged in contemporary popular media. If once a film or TV show permits, as an element of its diegesis, that nature is divorced from human life, it will be tempted to ascribe agency to natural forces. On the other hand, if the diegesis entails some order of continuity between physical and human nature, then the natural environment could be either the neutral presupposition of both kinds of life, mere context, or an agent whose will can be enacted in human biographies as well as the lives of animals and other natural forces. In all these scenarios, one thing remains the same: the communicative force of nature, whether that communication arises in the form of violence, of sharing or of care. One measure of the satisfactions of communication is the richness and complexity of its connections, as true of the shared grounds of human and biological life as it is of agency. Yet there will remain throughout the films discussed in this chapter the question of whether and to what extent either humans or the natural environment are free – free to act inside these dense networks of communication, or free of one another. The dramas act out a profound question concerning liberty: Must all organic creatures live and thrive only under the laws of nature, or does the probabilistic recognition of complexity and emergent orders endow the interconnected universe of the living with something akin to freedom, whether evolutionary (perhaps evolving towards higher orders of complexity) or directionless change?

Eco-economics

In Wolfgang Peterson's *The Perfect Storm* the ships setting out from Massachusetts into the long night that will destroy them are driven by economics. The trawler captains do not own their boats but lease them, and to keep them they have to bring in the fish. They have to set out so far from hope of landfall because the fish stocks are so severely depleted that the traditional voyages simply don't bring in sufficient tonnage, and they have to pursue the remaining shoals ever further into the open Atlantic. The storm itself is only one of the forces driving the men and women of the fishing fleet to destruction: the other is the capitalist system of ownership, loans and leasing. The great spiral formation of the weather system seems to imitate the omnivorous spiral of diminishing returns. Endless taking without return or respite could, in a more anthropomorphic film, be seen as the cause of the storm itself, the rage of nature ravaged beyond bearing. Peterson resists even the temptation to blame wider environmental pressures like global warming for the meteorological destiny that awaits his protagonists. Under the guiding hand of fate, the relentless pressure of the boat-owners shrivels to insignificance, the film focussing instead on the biographies of the swordboat men, their rugged lives, their dogged deaths.

The Perfect Storm is set in October of 1991. Two years earlier, Canadian fisheries minister John Crosbie, speaking in St John's, Nova Scotia, had tried to calm fears about a moratorium on cod fisheries. Eight months after the events depicted in the movie, he returned to announce the moratorium. In January 1994 the moratorium was extended. Mark Kurlansky, the historian of cod, comments:

> Canadian cod was not yet biologically extinct, but it was commercially extinct – so rare that it could no longer be considered commercially viable. Just three years short of the 500-year anniversary of the reports of [Genoese explorer John] Cabot's men scooping up cod in baskets, it was over. Fishermen had caught them all (Kurlansky 1997: 186).

The ecological collapse of the Grand Banks and the North Atlantic fisheries in general is an exemplary case of the effects of untrammelled exploitation of natural resources. The first industrial fisheries of the 19th century had been driven by Thomas Huxley's belief in the inexhaustible bounty of nature. The fate of the dodo might have pointed towards a different conclusion, as the neolithic extinctions of the megafauna of Old and New Worlds and Australia alike now show. But the demands of politics only ever take seriously the limitations of nature when those limitations are not only obvious but terminal. This I take to be the meaning of the phrase 'the tragedy of the commons' (Hardin 1968), the principle that what belongs to everyone, and should be everyone's care, is no-one's obligation and stands therefore to be squandered. Like Hegel's negative freedom, common ownership, in this conceptualisation, will always lead to common despoliation on the model of the common land which, the theory goes, was destroyed by overgrazing among the English peasantry.

In the case of the North Atlantic fisheries, the 'eco' in economics comes into play. Dwindling tonnage and fish size in the cod fishery is blamed on non-human predators, leading to the infamous Newfoundland seal cull. Meanwhile dwindling stocks raise prices and diminish demand, so that the fishermen move to other species, often the bait fish eaten by the dwindling cod, thus stopping population booms among fish deprived of predators, but also depriving the remaining cod of their food supply, while also risking, with smaller-gauge nets, catching many other fish that have to be thrown back, dead, into the sea. The boats are increasingly in debt to both government agencies extending loans and to the ordinary system of mortgages, so that fishing as an industry loses its rationale as provider of food and becomes instead a bureaucratic and fiscal regime whose purpose is to employ fishermen. One claim made by Massachusetts fishing communities is that subsidies are essential to maintain the skills of their trade until the fish return. At the same time, the increasing rate of technological development in fishing has radically altered those skills even in the fifty years since World War Two. Yet, according to UN Food and Agricultural Organisation figures, only a quarter of the world's fish stocks are underexploited: 47 per cent are maximally exploited, 18 per cent overexploited and 10 per cent 'have become significantly depleted, or are recovering from depletion and are far less productive than they used to be. Of particular concern is the failure of the stocks of haddock, redfish and cod to respond to the drastic management efforts that have been adopted in the North West Atlantic' (FAO 2002: 23). Nonetheless, total catches in the Northwest Atlantic have only halved since 1970, indicating that the fleets now trawl for other species: game fish, shellfish and erstwhile bait fish.

But then again, the data in Sebastian Junger's book, which inspired the movie, is telling. The establishment of Economic Exclusion Zones, the 200-mile limits over continental shelves, started a boom in the New England fisheries. Between 1976 and 1979 the fleet doubled to 1,300 boats. By the mid-80s 700 of them were swordfish boats using thirty- to forty-mile long monofilament lines, radar, satellite, electronic fish finders and temperature-depth gauges. In a scant five years, from 1987 to 1991, the year of *The Perfect Storm*, the swordfish catch fell from 45 to 33 million pounds weight, and average size from 165 to 110 pounds (Junger 1997: 81-6). Quotas were finally introduced in 1991. As Junger summarises their effects on the fishers, 'The result was that not only were fishing boats now racing the season, they were racing each other' (Junger 1997: 86). And in this instance, instead of pursuing the inexhaustible bounty of nature, they would be pursued by its inexhaustible wrath. Nonetheless, the instigating motive for the tale of *The Perfect Storm*, despite its title, is not meteorological apocalypse but biological.

Although there is also the question of why hundred-year weather events seem to occur with increasing frequency. The towering waves of that October storm may have been all the larger for the diminishing quantities of plankton in the North Atlantic, plankton that emit a chemical which, like oil, tends to calm the uppermost layer of water and stops the wind getting a wave-forming purchase on it. And global climate change may well have played on the three factors that built the storm: an unusually fierce Arctic low, a fluctuation in the jet stream, and a hurricane travelling far to the north of their usual grounds. Clearly however, even if the massive complexity of the chains linking overfishing to global warming could be nailed down causally, the chance that it might specify the crew of the *Andrea Gail* is unlikely. The meteorological storm crashes into the economic storm, and to a certain extent the political storm of quotas and fisheries management, the FAO and the WTO. The whole system is indistinguishably both social and environmental. In the crisis of the storm, the coincidence of the two is only more visible than, in calmer weather, it is in the trading of Lloyds maritime insurance. But is there freedom here? Or to start a little further down the chain, is there agency in a system which encompasses the global market in fish and at least a hemisphere of weather? The ways in which a film tells us a story about our condition in the face of nature is a barometer of sorts, a measurement of the atmospheric pressure in a culture that confronts an armageddon without magical solution.

For Hegel, 'absence of dependence on an other is won not outside the other but in it, [freedom] attains actuality not by fleeing the other but by overcoming it' (Hegel 1971: ¶ 382A). In Alan Wood's account, this means that Hegelian freedom should be understood as 'actively relating to something other than oneself in such a way that this other becomes integrated into one's projects, completing and fulfilling them so that it counts as belonging to one's own action rather than standing over against it' (Editor's Introduction to Hegel 1991: xii). In the *Philosophy of Right*, that other is the social world, civil society, the 'ethical life'. But the dialectical sense of a freedom which is gained by at once submitting to and subsuming the other can also be applied, as it is by Bookchin, to the subsumption of nature into human freedom. The reverse then might also be the case: that, as a communicative system, the eco-economic subsumes the human into its own freedom. Freedom then is maintained as a principle, but removed from the ancient and still in some ways sacrosanct notion that liberty is the unique property of the hairless biped. Systems do not abide by the linear causality espoused by Kant when he insisted on the antinomy of causality and freedom. Instead they come closer to his mentor Hume, whose famous 'fork' suggests that either the world is ordered on a causal basis and we have no free will, or the world is random, in which case we have no free will either, since whatever we do will have no causal relation to what comes after. Not even the overdetermination isolated by Louis Althusser (1965) in his anti-Hegelian revision of Marxism entirely accounts for systems. Certainly multiple causalities impact on any single event, but they do not necessarily cause the event in a linear way. Indeed, the event itself conspires with dialectical thought in the sense that it is not intrinsically self-identical either.

Where is the storm? Is it in the geographical bounds of a million square miles of North Atlantic? Or is it a perturbation that includes the entire economic and meteorological cycles of the planet? Is the storm only the storm, or is it a symptom? A symptom, that is, in the manner of Freudian slips, an epiphenomenon whose antecedent structures only emerge in the form that they do because they are ignored; or in the style of a reflex action, a spasm without consciousness, whose entire operation is preconscious, as the operations of the optic nerve or the gagging reflex. Shaped by uncountable numbers of molecular collisions, the very type of the emergent system, the storm multiplies causalities by powers of other causes in a bewildering mathematical paroxysm which is on the one hand utterly unmasterable, and on the other in thrall to its own composition. What terrible freedom it has is in any case brief, though harrowing; at best a temporary autonomous zone. Is that temporary organisation of the air and sea an entity?

Water

What does the film say? It describes the storm in a number of ways, often in the same shot. As the full 75 foot mock-up of the trawler *Andrea Gail* tosses on its gimbel on Warner Bros. sound stage 16, in a tank containing huge quantities of water set into a roll by wave-makers, cascades of water thunder from dump tanks and water cannon fire across the deck where the core action is taking place. The whole activity, itself a hammering physical test for the actors and crew, is performed in front of a huge 360-degree blue screen cyclorama. Onto this blue, the technicians from Industrial Light and Magic will composite their own confections of waves too dangerous for the largest ocean-going craft, in any case an unrepeatable fury of the elements, taking place in a night thickened with typhoon clouds, when there is so much water in the air that swimmers drown at the surface, and which therefore cannot be filmed. Yet this tale, based on a true story, yearns for the reality of the event, the irrecoverable terror of the six swordboat men and the incomprehensibly big seas of October 1991. Of course the script takes liberties with Junger's book, but every episode is a tale Junger has gleaned from his sources in Gloucester: clambering along a spar to cut the birds with welding gear; the shark grabbing a crewman by the leg; the wind snatching plywood sheets as the crew struggle to bolt them over the shattered windows of the wheelhouse. Location shoots in Gloucester itself, with Gloucester extras and cast members living in the bar where they will be filmed, are a token of the struggle for reality. But something here is too vast, too unique, and just too dark for cinematography. There is no way to reconstruct the events of the narrative without special effects. Once again, the ultimate in nature demands the ultimate in technology.

It is important to get beyond the marvellous to understand what exactly is happening here. Water is famously difficult to trick. It works very differently at different scales, an effect of surface tension, viscosity, reflectivity and the different behaviour of ripples and waves. Storm waters act differently again, keeping their mass and density in waves, but also frothing as they mix with hurricane winds, filling the air with foam, spray, spindrift. The storm has to be portrayed not only as volumes but as particles, which have dynamics close to but different from fluids. Some of the horror of that night, in Junger's account, derives from the night itself: the impossibility of rescue in the dark, the fading hope of rescue that might come after first light; the fathomless darkness of the deep as it were risen to the surface of the ocean. Virtual lightning and fields of digital moonlight are essential to make the invisible visible, which is after all what the film is attempting to do, albeit at the cost of verisimilitude.

To reprise an earlier argument, this is not a case of the sublime, a term which is designed to render the spectacle incommunicable. Film is a communication. What it communicates by definition cannot be sublime. Kant's and Burke's sublime, moreover, acts to preserve the realm of the divine apart from the merely human. Nature in its majesty is held up as the expression of inhuman divinity. But to the extent that the divine is necessary, the first cause, and determined by its existence, it cannot be free. What is remarkable about a storm as vast as this is that it is a process whose determinations are unfathomable, not because of their simplicity, their essence, but precisely because, in their complexity, there is nothing essential. The sublime, as that which by *force majeur* overwhelms the human, demeans meaning and irrationalises the rational. In this sense it is merely the obverse of evil, the irrational and meaningless exercise of power. Nancy, who sails close to essentialism in his Heideggerian emphasis on Being, nonetheless makes clear the stakes in the sublime when he describes the possibility of evil as 'the free renunciation of freedom' (Nancy 1993: 16), arguing that modernity is marked by just this renunciation, 'when the essence, concentrated in itself, of a process, of an institution (technical, social, cultural, political) prevents existence from existing, that is to say from acceding to its proper essence' (Nancy 1993: 17).

For us, the storm is not an essence but a process; for an essence, despite Nancy's arguments to the contrary, determines its phenomenon. Systemic thought sees the world as process, but agrees with Nancy's definition of evil where an institution, in some broad sense of the term, amasses, delays, diverts or blocks the flows that make up systemic process and piles them into a dam. The sublime is such a dam, a mode of thought destined to refuse all other thoughts than itself. In its place, what the perfect storm and *The Perfect Storm* suggest is wonder, that emotional, visceral subsumption of the otherness of the other in its microscopic particularity, its rigourously unique configuration. Where the sublime testifies to unchanging deity, wonder accedes to the instant, the moment of disappearance and becoming, the singularity of any perception, when one perception bursts through the bonds of habit. Far from annihilating language, wonder demands that language reopen itself to possibilities for which it has no lexicon or syntax, that it be renewed. Renewal clearly indicates a temporal dimension of process. The sublime is outside of time; beauty embraces the sensory evidence of time's passage; but wonder thrills to its perpetual emergence. The sublime makes thinking unthinkable by removing from it what thinking has in place of freedom: thought's openness to change, and thus to any kind of future. Wonder is the very possibility of thinking, not its antithesis. It is an assertion of the integration of humanity into the world, or more specifically, the experience which, in confronting a person with their world, confronts the world with that person. In some intense detail or some vast panorama, wonder no longer permits us to perceive ourselves apart from the world, or or to believe that the world is inhuman. Reversing Hegel, wonder is the principle according to which the world subsumes the human into itself, and doing so makes possible humanity, as a time-based process of thinking and a collective and systemic process of speaking what is thought: a polis.

In the 21st century, however, inhumanity can no longer be distinguished from the eco-economic cycles of human integration into the natural world. The crew of the *Andrea Gail* are there not for their own causes but in the service of the boat-owner and his mortgage, articulated with the banking and finance sector as much as the fluctuating market for marine protein. The movie assembles from Junger a series of accidents that deprive the swordboat of its communications: the storm fills the FM waveband with static, rips away the antennae, sets the GPS awash. Deep sea fishermen, for all that they can be pilloried by pious environmentalists, are as close as we get to the human integrated into their ecology, not just as predators, but as the cunning navigators of an ever-changing dimension. Stripped of the network technologies that keep them alive but, in the same moment, keep them in hock to the eco-economics of their work, their climactic struggle for survival is about their practical knowledge of their vessel, their ability to work together, their willingness to take on the storm.

Billy Tine (George Clooney, top left) at the helm of the *Andrea Gail* in the dump tank. *The Perfect Storm* Courtesy British Film Institute

In the three-minute sequence of the *Andrea Gail*'s turn, a decision made to survive rather than to race the storm to port, there are 52 shots, giving an average shot length just over three seconds. Among the longer shots is a steadicam of the cabin with the four crew, and four vignette portraits of each of the below-deck crewmen running at four seconds apiece. Among the faster shots are a series of cutaways of Billy and Bobby's faces and hands as they struggle to turn the ship. Surprisingly, given the unwritten rule against allowing effects shots to run longer than necessary and so risk discovering their artifice, the long shot composites of the *Andrea Gail* and surrounding waves run for the most part slightly over the average. Although the low light levels help hide some of the digital plates, the lightning flashes, which occupy up to ten frames, show a lot of detail. Meanwhile the physical effects (ie those produced by physical devices rather than CGI), not only the water washing into the deckhouse but the spattered droplets on the windows, work as powerfully as the wetted hair to push a sense of the physical reality of the scene. Compositing the interior with digital effects, favouring the screen-left window behind Billy, is enhanced with foreground spray and drips, building the scene in layers that emphasise the space in which the drama is played out, the fragile interior, the vast outside. Synchronisation of CGI and physical effects, more difficult than usual to achieve because of the need to deploy underwater cameras in the wheelhouse set, is even harder when the entire set is shaken by a sudden dump of water, so that the CGI has to match the shaken camera. Nonetheless there is a surprising depth of field to these shots, in contrast to the close-ups of Billy and Bobby, where the background is thrown out of focus to favour nuances of performance, but also to detail the physical battering the characters have taken.

Habib Zargarpour, effects supervisor for the film at ILM, was responsible for both the wave and the digital *Andrea Gail* that tries to ride it. Using reference footage from the US Coastguard for the bow spray and the wave surfaces as well as their mass and motion, the digital team tried at every stage for convincing images, but even more for images that would not be attractive as effects but as elements of a visual narrative; in short, for realism. The sound design is similarly realist, especially in its synchronisation and sweetening of the gaps between live and digital action. But the sound is a more symbolic element here, especially the moaning of wind in the rigging, a theme emphasised in Junger's book, as it is in most descriptions of the Beaufort scale, a recreation of actuality that takes on an allegorical or musical function. The over-emphatic orchestral score aggressively subordinates the storm to the emotional life of the characters, and works in a direction directly antagonistic to the themes of the film, at least where they are at their most ecologically rich: the smallness of even the strongest emotions in the face of such extreme moments, when the natural world no longer conforms to expectations, and all other dreams pass into the night. The thin echoes of the already reed-thin death scene of *Titanic* is unmistakable in Bobby's farewell, the motif of undying love a palliative that diminishes the film's potential to communicate the natural world's autonomy, just as it was in Cameron's film.

The ocean seen from shore, the dripping and pouring of rain, wet hair and clothing are familiar stuff. The titanic waves of *The Perfect Storm* are of a far more alien kind. A Hollywood film has to personify its characters as individual psychologies – films do not get financed otherwise. But to his credit Peterson resists the temptation to personify the storm itself. In the 'false dawn' scene that follows, Billy remarks, 'It's not going to let us go', attributing agency to the storm, but not personality. Only the final wave gets to be called 'bitch', more a last entry into Billy's psychology than nomination, and as nomination restricted to the monster wave alone, not the storm as a whole. In scenes shot in the NBC weather room set, the storm is a meteorological object or concatenation of objects, lacking even the nomenclature provided for the tropical storm Grace that contributes to it. It is instead a collision of money and meteorology with the lives of the film's protagonists. Coastguards, the Crow's Nest community back in Gloucester, and the yacht crew form a counterpoint to the *Andrea Gail*, but never face what the fishermen do, subsumption into the storm, becoming elemental vectors of the wind and waves, throwing in their lot, unwilling, fighting, creating possibilities.

The others can be treated with professional sentimentality: the bantering flirtation between Billy and the woman skipper, the play on dreams, the doting father's obsequiously precocious son. The shreds of Junger's informants still survive somewhere under the gloss. But their role is as supporting chorus to the central tragedy, which is that of the ship's captain, not overly prepossessing, especially when he is given an out-of-character speech about the joys of his job, and even more so when the speech is repeated as the voice-over for his putative lover's memories. In short, the film has all the vices of Hollywood. But it has too that scrap of enlightenment that keeps us watching at least some of Hollywood's productions, some scenes and sequences of distracting honesty and perspective. Most of all these are scenes of action and environment, especially the actions of working men in vigourous pursuit of a profession they know in their blood, and an environment which increasingly is indistinguishable from it. Their freedom is the freedom to become the element they battle, not by submitting but exactly by pitching themselves in life-and-death struggle against the element, allowing themselves to be subsumed in it. It is the realisation of a different Hegel (1977: 111-119): the Hegel of the master-slave dialectic, and the bitter purchase of freedom.

Hegel stands accused, by such opposing thoughts as those of Marx and Popper, of tyranny, the triumph of a model over historical, social and cultural difference. This is, in some ways, the core of the master-slave (or lord and bondsman) dialectic of the *Phenomenology*. Faced with another self-consciousness, the self is forced to come out of itself. Each of these selves sees at once itself and otherness in the self that faces it; each attempts to subsume the other into itself, to be the one that recognises, rather than the one that is recognised. On this primal scene of a battle of wills depends the freedom of the self, for, says Hegel (1977: 114), 'The individual who has not risked his life may well be recognised as a *person*, but he has not attained to the truth of this recognition as an independent self-consciousness', an independence which can only be won by subsuming the otherness of the other into the self, an act that can only be achieved by one of the parties, and at the expense of the other. The loser, in what Hegel sees as a life-or-death struggle, is condemned to entanglement in relationships, unable to step out of them into pure being-for-self. The winner becomes such a being-for-self, while the loser has to work manufacturing, out of raw reality, the objects of his lord's desires. But as a result, the stuff of reality only has genuine independence for the one who works it, who gives it form, and therefore permanence, and who achieves his own independence in the autonomy of the world. The lord meanwhile is deprived of this essential relation: everything he desires is mediated through the nonetheless unvalued other, the bondsman. The loser wins, and the winner loses. This dialectic devolves upon the fear of death, and its overcoming. The winner of the struggle is the one who accepts the possibility, even the certainty, of his own death, and in so doing achieves freedom. Once the necessity that the competing other be human is removed, we have the skeletal outline of *The Perfect Storm*: men who accept mortality and nonetheless fight to the death to overcome its bearer achieve a fearful freedom, a freedom which, however, can never be celebrated.

In effect, like Hegel's dialectic of the lord and bondsman, the crew, and chief among them Billy Tyne, achieve a fundamental paradox which in Hegel was a resolution of a moment of the dialectic: freedom is destiny. The pleonasm, with the memory of the European dictatorships of the mid-20th century still fresh in mind, has today darker connotations. The 'free renunciation of freedom' that Nancy discovered in modernity is echoed in Bauman's discussion, deriving from Max Scheler, of the difference between fate and destiny. 'Fate is not a matter of free choice, and particularly of the individual free choice', argues Bauman (2000: 210): it grows out of biography and society, out of an unexamined life. 'To understand one's fate means to be aware of its difference from one's destiny', he continues, 'And to understand one's fate is to know the complex network of causes that brought about that fate and its difference from that destiny' (Bauman 2000: 212). Billy Tyne's speech about the joys of being a swordboat captain is exactly such a failure to examine the conditions which bring a man to a specific fate, which is why it appears so gauche and sentimental as dialogue, and even more so as voice-over coda to the film. Both book and film of *The Perfect Storm* make a point of respecting the traditions of Gloucester, framing the narrative with pans over the memorial wall for those lost at sea and the town's waterfront statue of a fisherman (excoriated by Charles Olson, long time resident of the town, in his poem *Maximus* as 'that awful sculpture'). But those 'traditions' are illusory, the product of profound changes to fishing technology and to the fertility of the neighbouring seas in the lifetime of the *Andrea Gail*'s crew. Though the real crew may well have known far more about why they sailed that October, the film denies them an examination of all that conditions their lives, reducing their deaths to fates. Properly tragic, the struggle to the death that they engage against nature, stripped of its social and eco-economic conditions, is reduced to a necessity boldly faced. Neither the will of God nor cosmic justice are in play, still less the forces of political economy. 'They took their impious risks and died', as MacDiarmid wrote: the moment that in Hegel forms a beginning is in the conditions of contemporary capital literally a dead end.

Mending Rope

Niki Caro's adaptation of Witi Ihimaera's novel *The Whale Rider* works in the very different context of a traditional society confronting change. Both the adaptation and the cut scenes evidence a reluctance to address in much detail either the social effects of colonisation on Maori communities in rural Aotearoa, or the political awareness that gradually dawns on the novel's narrator, Rawiri, whose appearance in the film is largely restricted to comic relief. Instead the film emphasises destiny, a continuity with the past which nonetheless leaves open the chance to make a choice. Maori speak of 'travelling into the future facing backwards', of consulting with the ancestors on the proper way to move ahead. Here the crux of the issue is a break in the patrilineal handing on of responsibility for the tradition with the birth of a girl-child in place of the expected eldest son. In the opening sequence, underwater footage looking up into the surface of the sea cuts to a traumatic birth. An insert shot, stock footage of a southern wright whale emerging to vision through murky water, echoes the infant's navigation of the birth canal before cutting back to often distorted and distended shots of mother's face cross-fading into her baby daughter's. Over these, Paikea's commentary doubles the analogy between her birth and the arrival of her ancestor, the first Paikea, to Whangara aboard the whale. Beneath her voice-over, Lisa Gerrard's score begins with a conch, adding gongs and the upward keening of a shell flute, as long chords in the string section stretch across the two times of the film's world, the time of the ancestors and contemporary life on the East Cape of New Zealand's North Island, Te Tai Rawhiti. The same theme will reappear in the climactic scene when Paikea gives the bull whale the traditional greeting of a hungi, a sharing of breath, before climbing onto its back, stitching together the ancient and the contemporary.

The film, expensive by the standards of Aotearoa New Zealand, was obliged to drop much of what makes Ihimaera's novel so redolent of its place, the everyday mixture of Te Reo, Maori speech, with English. The traditional instruments refer international audiences to the tradition in the way that the language does in the novel, where the whales converse in Te Reo. (Conversely, in the novel Paikea sings wordlessly to the whales where in the film she chants in Te Reo). And likewise the whales 'interlock' (to use Ihimaera's word, 1987: 147) between natural and supernatural, as between ancient and contemporary worlds, as befits another of the film's key themes, the continuity between tangata whenua, the people of the land, and the natural environment. The break that Koro, guardian of tradition, fears, the break of the bloodline, is also the break he dreads when he asks the dying whale 'Who is to blame?'. And as Paikea mends the broken rope, which Koro has used to explain the continuity and strength of the ancestors, so she is charged with remaking the ancestral unity with the whales. 'He wanted to die. There wasn't a reason to live anymore' says Paikea in voiceover, on a cut from her to Koro in the surf by the whale, identified now, as in the novel, as the original Paikea's whale, who has flexed his great flukes to break the would-be rescuers' rope – again that image of ancestral bonds untangling. The small adumbrations of untyings – Hemi's father's retreat from the marae to his rocker bros; Rawiri's mates trying to leave the school concert, or Rawini's bag of dope on his recumbent belly – all converge on this unravelling. Koro has settled for fate.

And yet the film is quite clearly articulated around destiny, a difficult remaking of the tradition around a woman. There is a brief mention in dialogue of Muriwai when Nanny Flowers mentions her ancestor, an ancestor who broke the ban on women speaking on the marae, and who lifted her skirts there to remind the men of where they came from. Paikea has come also from that lineage and that shocking honesty about natural processes (faintly echoed in the film's joke about smoking and reproduction). So her remaking of the tradition in a new way, that encompasses the female element, is in accordance with history, but a history re-examined for what it can bring that is new. The short documentary 'Te Waka - Building the Canoe' included on the DVD release notes that the boat's carvers laid a male pattern down one flank, and a female down the other, uniting them in the whale motifs of the prow and stern. Though for reasons of cost and speed, the waka was far from traditional in construction, its development of the film's themes in a neo-traditional medium indicates something of the flexibility of a traditional culture whose circumstances constantly require it to question the ancestors for advice on unprecedented dilemmas.

There is a minor discontinuity in the movie. After the beaching, Paikea wakes. Her gaze from her window cuts to a reverse angle on eighteen or so whales – the fibreglass models built for the show by Duncan Major, also production designer for *The Lord of the Rings*, but also a number of digital whales added to the composite. A previous shot of the same beach had only ten or so, albeit from a slightly different angle associated with Rawiri's point of view. Not surprisingly, the wide shot reversing Nanny Flower's gaze at Paikea riding the whale into the surf also features CGI whales added to the cinematic plate. These shots, running at close to three seconds, all in wide shot and deep focus, are subtle additions, especially the beach scene, where the activities of the people of Whangara, working as extras in their own story, occupies most of the central field and, for this viewer at least, most of a spectator's attention. That elision, that near-voluntary blindness, is indicative of values that drive the film's ecological concerns, while once again weaving together technological and natural to place and privilege a story which, even more than personal, concerns the remaking of polis.

The document of the local people tending the whales exceeds the CGI, and the emotional impact of the scene, the performances of the extras and the vivid presence of the sea, the tides and the coastward hills move attention from the false whales to their position in the narrative, that is their relation to the humans around them. Perhaps this might be seen as reversing the infamous trick pulled by Flaherty, when he got the old men of Arran to teach the young how to whale from long boats. As with Flaherty's *Man of Arran*, one has the impression not of fiction but of re-enactment, beachings being, sadly, not at all uncommon on Aotearoa's coasts. Re-enactment, and re-enchantment. As Koro realises simultaneously that Paikea is the one and that he has lost her, the camera dollies in towards him, the background of dune grasses and grassy hills drifting only slightly out of focus. The place, its thousand-year history, rediscovers itself in the instant that Koro recognises the strange shape that time has chosen for the return of the ancestor. It is a kind of gestalt, a moment not of crisis but in which the past gathers itself into a single realisation, as when you understand a sentence in a foreign language only after it has all been said, in one sudden flash summing up the fragmentary understandings you had of individual words beforehand.

The contrast between this historical deliberation – Paikea's absorbed gaze into the frayed rope – and the lack of anything similar in *The Perfect Storm* – is not intended to distinguish Hollywood from independent filmmaking, or Western modernity from traditional society, but to indicate the tendencies of ecological thought. Bauman recalls Thoreau's metaphor of skating on thin ice: in risky situations, speed is your ally. But then you are entirely at the mercy of a world of risk which you did not create. To the immense frustration of modernisers in Aotearoa New Zealand, tangata whenua, the people of the land, often require long counsel and meticulous working-through before accepting change. Yet the pause to examine options, however thin the ice appears to those shouting 'Hurry!' from the banks, is one way to make sure you do not skate into open water and drown. All too often, ecological thought presents itself politically as the annunciation of catastrophe, of ecological armageddon moments away from occurring, and demanding instantaneous action. Yet that mode of thinking is all too close both to the radical authoritarianism of fascist politics, always premised on the need for authority to avert crisis, and to the ordinary fatalism of corporate globalisation. In traditional societies, taking the time for thought is equivalent to what, in contemporary theory, emerges as the necessity for exile.

In Vilém Flusser's (2003) account, the migrant, willing or not, is forced out into a void, where meaning can no longer arise from habit or habitus. The bewildering moment can be handled in one of a number of ways. The migrant can cling to the home culture as an idealised vision – the culture of the expatriate. Or she can use the wrench into disorientation to claim freedom from the past and a new, ironic gaze upon both the home culture and the new place where she arrives. Flusser does not say, but it is I think legitimate to argue, that this 'freedom from' is that patrician, aristocratic view from the mountain tops espoused by Nietzsche and Bataille. What Flusser does say is that 'freedom from' is only half a freedom, and as such unfree. What remains is for the migrant to seize the ironic moment of liberty and commit herself to using it in the context of the culture where she lands. Only in that engagement with change, that grasping of responsibility, does the migrant achieve her freedom. 'The dialogic spirit that characterises exile may not be one of mutual recognition; it is mostly polemical and even murderous' (Flusser 2003: 87): in the far rougher vision of Ihimaera's novel, Koro utterly rejects Paikea, and some of that emotional violence remains in scenes of the film, like that where Koro breaks a cup pounding on the tabletop.

Koro's time, and the time that Paikea must spend to make him understand, are not durations that can be cut short. Like the migrant's exile in space, though the time be painful, it is only by refusing the stasis of place or the instantaneity of crisis-management that it is possible to undo the mistaking of destiny for fate. Unlike *The Perfect Storm*, *Whale Rider* describes the stubborn lack of communication that arises from the clash of wills, and provides, in the arrival of the whales, a quite different interlock. Here there is little question of rights, and much about obligations, responsibilities, duties. The western tradition of political modernity has thought of freedom, especially in film, as a perquisite of action movies. Freedom is associated with doing, with decisions swiftly made and swiftly realised. But the long rhythms and complex connectivities of ecological thinking do not bear that kind of crisis-thinking, nor the brutal confrontation of nature against humanity in a life-or-death struggle in which one or the other is destroyed. Neither Caro's film nor Ihimaera's novel offers global answers: they deal with the intensely local: with a single family in a remote community. Their solutions may not be generalised. But the film's rejection of confrontation, and with it the tragedy of destiny, builds its hope on such small foundations. Here freedom no longer belongs to the hero but to a whole world.

Commenting on the lord and bondsman dialectic in series of lectures given between 1933 and 1939 and attended, among others, by Jacques Lacan, Alexandre Kojève diffuses the heroism and tragedy to produce an adumbration of systems theory:

> Human Desire must be directed toward another Desire. For there to be human Desire, then, there must first be a multiplicity of (animal) Desires . . . That is why the human reality can only be social. But for the herd to become a society, multiplicity of Desires is not sufficient by itself: in addition the Desires of each member of the herd must be directed – or potentially directed

> – toward the Desires of the other members. If the human reality is a social reality, society is human only as a set of Desires mutually desiring one another as Desires (Kojève 1969: 5-6)

Rather than focus on the fight to the death, Kojève isolates desire as desire for the desire of the other. It is true that Kojève rests his case on the distinction between animal (immediate) and social (mediated) desire. But in the years since World War Two, increasingly, and in *Whale Rider* specifically, the desire of the whales and that of the ancestors is equally implicated in the desires of the human family at the core of the drama. These questions of continuities, of communicating with and giving to the green world, will involve us in explorations of tradition and the presence of ancestors (Chapter 7 below). First, however, we need to understand some other popular mediations of key features in the life of the polis: death, struggle and isolation.

Edge of Darkness

EcoTerrorism and the Public Sphere

We are always conquering Nature, because 'Nature' is the name for what we have, to some extent, conquered
(CS Lewis, *The Abolition of Man,* 1955: 83)

Kant on Social Realism

The BBC TV drama series *Edge of Darkness*, first broadcast in 1985, was one of the last times public service television undertook a major intervention in political drama with such seriousness and such ratings success. BBC Worldwide have made it available on DVD; director Martin Campbell, whose recent credits include *GoldenEye* (1995), *The Mask of Zorro* (1998) and *Vertical Limit* (2000), is rumoured to be in preproduction with a feature film version. The moment of *Edge of Darkness* was one of bewilderment on the Left. The series made its mark not only through its politics, a tale of government conspiracy, nuclear risk and ecopolitical direct action, but because it lived these themes through the eyes of a bereft parent for whom the world had already ended. Searching for a reason to do politics in the face of despair, the series neatly echoed the chill that descended on radical politics in the Thatcher years in the United Kingdom, but also that hinge between despair and desperation that levers terrorism into existence. That it was television rather than cinema that voiced this desperate politics raises the question of the public sphere, and the different claims of the individual, the public, the nation, the country and the land to a stake in the life of the polis.

The pages of *Screen* were among those inhabited by a growing concern that arguments on behalf of the public service remit of the BBC were defending the indefensible: that a paternalistic and ultimately governmental authority was scarcely worth preserving, even if the promised alternative was far worse. Beachheads established in the new UK Channel 4, launched in 1981, seemed to promise that even in commercial environments, quality, however defined, and alternative voices could still find distribution. Of course it was not Channel 4's cultural remit but its economics of publishing that fired the monetarist imagination. The Home Office Committee on Financing the BBC, chaired by Professor Alan Peacock (generally referred to as the Peacock Committee), was established in the mid-1980s to explore the possibilities for advertising, sponsorship and other income-generating schemes, reporting in 1986, narrowly heading off an advertising-based economic model on the grounds that this would eat into the financial viability of the existing commercial channels, already smarting from the competition of Channel 4 and the emergence of direct broadcasting by satellite (Barnett and Doherty 1986). Perhaps as a result, 1985 appears in retrospect as the end of a golden age of television drama in the UK. In subsequent years, only *Our Friends from the North* and *State of Play* came close to the commitment and edginess of the mid-1980s, while Dennis Potter's signature, the gold standard of highbrow TV productions in subsequent years, was affixed to more and more self-indulgent exercises in style the higher his critical star rose. *Edge of Darkness* belongs to a brief moment, prior to the multichannel world and the more deferential politics of later TV drama, when broadcast drama could still think of itself as creating space for public debate.

A key task of TV drama, John Caughie reminds us, is the production of space. Especially in the viewing situation typical of UK television in the 1980s, the living room screen was the dominant site of audiencing. The programme's first task was to create a space that might articulate the determining spaces of domesticity and felt reality with the undetermined spaces of fiction in such a way as to permit a political discourse. While tentative about identifying the living room context as a formal characteristic distinguishing television from other media (novel reading has always been subject to the same interruptions), Caughie does give a strong statement of social realist television drama's Lefebvrean construction of space:

> Characters . . . function , in the Lukacsian sense, as points of condensation for the social and historical, and what connects them to the social is the space in which they circulate. Space, that is to say, is not simply the space of narrative action but is the contextual space of social history; it is not simply at the service of narrative but is the point of contact to a reality outside the narrative, there in its own right, and giving the narrative its social significance – its 'seriousness' (Caughie 2000: 135)

In Caughie's reading, the space of social realism navigates between the possible, that is to say that which can be imagined *mentally* in accordance with what we intuit and conceive about the world, and the real, that which can be *sensed.* The audiovisual media must always traverse this movement, since their distinguishing feature is that they offer to the senses what otherwise, in literature for example, must be imagined. While a philosopher might ask us to conceive of a triangle, the audiovisual media present us with it as an object of perception. But the claim of social realism is greater than this. In the Lukacsian variant, the claim is for a condensation, in the social realist text, of historical process and historical law. Lukacs (1969) thus builds a bridge between the possible – the fictional – and the determined, the necessary, what exists above and beyond human imagination or human perception. For Lukacs then the otherwise invisible laws of history are responsible for the construction of space. For Lefebvre, some decades later, space would be socially constructed. But in certain senses, this vanguard conception of space as malleable performance is not yet available to the popular mediations of *Edge of Darkness*, whose world is closer to the earliest conceptions of space from the grounding moments of European republicanism in the philosophy of Immanuel Kant.

In Kant's Transcendental Aesthetic, time and space are given *a priori*, the necessary grounds on which all experience depends. Kant's geometric space-time is Euclidean, absolute extension and absolute duration underpinning and making possible all perceptions and understandings of them. That which does not occupy a place or change through time is in this sense beyond perception and understanding. In the Transcendental Doctrine of Judgement, Kant's job is to define the possibilities for knowledge about the world. To achieve this, he attempts to distinguish the limits of empirical or perceptually-based knowledge in the fit between intuition and perception and the determining role of time and space in establishing relations between entities. This produces the triple organisation of empirical thought into the possible, the real and the necessary, the categories of intuition, perception and existence. The second postulate is of special interest: 'That which coheres with the material conditions of experience (sensation) is *real*.' (Kant 1890: 161). The question of mediation appears not to have arisen in the first Critique, but for students of media, 'that which coheres with the material conditions of experience' surely includes, among other things, televisualisation. Fiction is, in Kant's sense, real when it coheres with the material conditions of experience. By giving those 'material conditions' a materialist spin, we have the basis for a definition of social realism, and one moreover that ties it directly to the nature of space, time and causality.

Few scholars today would care to defend Kant's idealist propositions on the absolute and universal nature of space, time or the sort of cause-effect relations that a universal standard grid makes possible. Where Kant provided for the reciprocity of substances sharing one space and one time, we begin to appreciate the coexistence of multiple space-times in a single event, including but not limited to Kant's Euclidean geometry of (and absolute distinction between) space and time. Nonetheless, and despite a general popular awareness of relativity, grids of longitude and latitude and the regular ticking of clock time still occupy the foreground of popular consciousness of time, not least in TV drama where deadlines and distance are regular script devices. Though *Edge of Darkness* features a protagonist apparently quite abstracted from clock time, its construction of social space depends on an awareness of geography and history as the conditions of drama and by implication of action. here it converges with the Enlightenment philosopher. The dimensions of space and time that undergird human experience also provide the foundations for Kant's universal Republicanism. The Eighth Thesis of Kant's 'Universal History with a Cosmopolitan Intent' asserts that 'One can regard the history of the human species, in the large, as the realization of a hidden plan of nature to bring about an internally, and for this purpose, also an externally perfect national constitution, as the sole state in which all of humanity's natural capacities can be developed' (Kant 1983: 36). The terrain on which a global and secure peace might be built is here defined in terms of a linear progression of history and a determinate geography of borders, public space conforming to the geometry and regularity of space and time defined in the *Critique of Pure Reason*.

In our time, that agora is only one of many overlapping and sometimes mutually exclusive and contradictory spaces. This, as I understand it, is Caughie's point about the contextual spaces of social history in narrative drama. Yet in many respects the geometry of the public *sphere*, and the normative critique established by Habermas (1984) that presumes a *goal* of communicative rationality, informs the work of committed TV drama with principles entirely compatible with Kant's foundations. Television drama had aspired, in the 1960s and 1970s, especially in the work of Loach, MacTaggart, McGrath, Griffiths and Watkins, to be such space of critique, debate and democracy in the interests of a progressive politics. To do so it used the intimacy and domesticity of the television receiver to recover and represent spaces of the world beyond the TV apparatus. Such spaces were themselves dual, both ordinary lived reality and the reality of the vast operations of history. In this sense *Edge of Darkness* takes us to a limit point of that articulation, layering together the sensuous reality of life in the living room with the more metaphysical grounds of the sweep of history. The programme can do so because it sits at a specific moment of television history in the UK. The question then is which public spaces were possible, and which were becoming possible or impossible in 1984-5 when the series was being conceived and produced?

Dimensions of the Public Sphere

The mise-en-scène of *Edge of Darkness* places us in offices and anonymous hotels, 'ordinary' flats and houses, linked by frequent passes over television screens to a contemporary newscape of miner's strikes and war. Exteriors are bustling streets, underground stations, and car interiors on motorways drenched in familiar rain, now with overdubbed radio broadcasts to intricate them into the public world of politics and trade: telephones, photocopiers and computers with command-line interfaces on ranks of desks under fluorescent light, a Westminster committee room, the crush bar at the Barbican. (A rare joke has a policeman radioing in that he followed the exit signs and found himself on the roof - reference to the notoriously labyrinthine passageways leading into and out of the City of London cultural venue). Much of the shoot is done in available light, much of it overcast daylight, little of it colour-corrected to cure the characters of their piscine, rain-washed pallor. More frequent and closer close-ups than usual even on TV, unenhanced by softening fills, inspect faces wearing little enough make-up to show the texture of shaving burns and flooded veins in actors' eyes. 16 mm film gives the image a granularity that somehow tunes to the rains and mists of the autumnal setting. In a number of external and crowd shots, the camera seems to have been placed well back from the action, with a zoom lens to bring characters close to the screen, in the process making the spaces shallow and flat, an effect doubled by the lighting codes. As a result, large blurred shapes of passers-by and fragments of cars or buses drag across the screen, obscuring the focused area where a key action or dialogue takes place. The soundtrack too keeps the roar of traffic as a major element of the mix, as actors raise their voices to be heard over the din of the street. *Edge of Darkness* director Martin Campbell and director of photography Andrew Dunn go to great lengths to give the drama not so much grit, a term with too many connotations in British social realism, as grain, a texture that forms the specific skin on which the political intrigue and the emotional drama can meet in a single space.

Protagonist Ronnie Craven (Bob Peck) rarely appears in warm tones, especially apposite since in some ways he is already dead. His only daughter for whom, there are numerous hints, he harbours incestuous yearnings, raised as the only child of an only parent after his wife's death from cancer, is murdered in the opening episode but comes back as a revenant to guide Craven on his quest. Only really alive when she appears, his major motivation is to preserve her memory and her returns, and only secondarily to find the truth about her death. Revenge only comes as a final thought, and it is not he who wreaks it. Craven's posthumous affectlessness is contrasted with Jedburgh (Joe Don Black), hard-drinking, fast-talking bon viveur. Craven seems to thrive on surfaces, on the tactile, his skin a pale bruise, his world reduced to the touch he offered as an interrogator of IRA suspects, and offers to the gunman McCroom who pulled the trigger on Emma (Joanne Whalley), his dead daughter. There are similarities with the cinematic style of *The Sixth Sense* and *Signs*.

Contradictions unearthed in debates on the Left over the Peacock committee, notably the defeatist recognition that protecting the BBC was a defence of state-sponsored paternalism, or at least a Hobson's choice between the powers of the state and the powers of capital, are intricately evolved in the narrative of *Edge of Darkness*. The doubled political-familiar and tactile-ghostly spaces must articulate with the real time of the living room, domestic flows of people, meals, pets and bedtimes. Unburdened by advertising breaks, at this stage not dependent on export and therefore not even designed to have ad breaks inserted at appropriately regular intervals, there is nonetheless a temporal imperative in the form of the episodic tradition of transmission, itself figured on a knowledge *supposed* to be true by the public service broadcaster (and therefore supposed to be knowledge) concerning its imaginary audience, its public: that it cannot bear very much fiction, and needs breaks from concentrated viewing. This unequal relation was the target of the most radical interventions in television production, but rarely popular outside the realms of comedy and satire.

In the paternalist model, the viewer is expected to suppose an authoritative subject somewhere on the further side of the screen, one moreover that is supposed to 'know', to possess an imaginary plenitude which the narrative will eventually deliver. The broadcaster meanwhile supposes a public that is in need of healing in a process which is either interminable or whose success would in any case bring about the end of the therapy – not only the end of the series but the end of television. The mutuality of this imaginary transference, between the one supposed to know and the one supposed to need knowledge, defines the bad faith of public service broadcasting, in which the broadcaster serves the public but no less the public serves the broadcaster. At the heart of this imagined national public lay a conflict between the civil citizen and the family member, with all the shadings of Oedipal scenarios that carried for a public service which was simultaneously the voice of public authority, and an authority that required defending from even more powerful forces. Thus the significance of the mise-en-scène, the diegesis and the camerawork, and to some extent the sound design of *Edge of Darkness* and their concern with the ruptured spaces of the family, held together by unnameable (and unacted) desires and torn apart by an external violence, itself product of Emma's mistaken belief that the nuclear waste of Northmoor was a political issue, when it turns out to be a crisis in the transition from state secrecy to commercial confidentiality. In the potential demise of paternalist public service, it seems to argue, what is at stake is not the death of the father, but the death of the dependent child: the audience. The series than must turn to address the possibilities for an audience that is no longer familial but public, and a television that sacrifices authority for debate. In doing so, it will however also risk losing the coherence of space and time on which the construction of a public sphere had thus far been built.

Similarly and in parallel, the series plots a transition from an older BBC rhetoric of care to the feared discourse of efficiency which seemed central to the fundamentally economic brief of the Peacock committee. Fred Inglis, in a succinct analysis of the series, offers this quote from

Raymond Williams, published two years before the first broadcast, to describe the political shift of the Thatcher years on which Peacock's new brief was premised, where 'Plan X' is a playful term for the cold wind of managerialism in the then Conservative government:

> Plan X is sharp politics and high-risk politics. It is easily presented as a version of masculinity. Plan X is a mode of assessing odds and of determining a game plan . . . To emerge as dominant it has to rid itself, in practice, of whatever covering phrases may be retained, of still powerful feelings and habits of mutual concern and responsibility . . . At the levels at which Plan X is already being played, in nuclear arms strategy, in high-capital advanced technologies, in world-market investment policies, and in anti-union strategies, the mere habits of struggling and competing individuals and families, the mere entertainment of ordinary gambling, the simplicities of local and national loyalties . . . are in quite another world. Plan X, that is to say, is by its nature not for everybody. It is the emerging rationality of self-conscious élites . . . it is its emergence as the open common sense of high-level politics which is really serious. As distinct from mere greedy muddle, and from shuffling day-to-day management, it is a way – a limited but powerful way – of grasping and attempting to control the future. (Williams 1983: 248)

A secret that is no longer secretive, replacing the paternalist with the efficiency model of public service broadcasting under Plan X implies the reconception of television not as a field of public debate but as a medium for promoting or denying the 'oxygen of publicity'. (One thinks instantly of Thatcher's revenge on Thames TV, whose loss of franchise was widely rumoured to be a direct result of the company's insistence on screening the drama-doc *Death of a Princess*).

Plan X relies on the open secret, the disavowal of treachery in a knowing and ironic pleasure in pulling one over in plain sight. The revelations of *Edge of Darkness* are that there are no revelations: someone always knows, some agency has already been alerted, some greater conspiracy, itself wide open to a public scrutiny it never receives, always engulfs the small trickeries that the programme's protagonists engineer. Unlike US television's federal government paranoia cycle (starting with *The X Files*), there is no Big Lie. The tools are always to hand for unveiling the vicious and the self-interested, but because their motives are so transparent, their means so familiar and their goals so banal, an already disillusioned audience reacts with something like Craven's jaded fatalism. Only the detail counts: that Emma was murdered 'by accident'.

It is this flaw in the gameplay that irks; not, in the end, the game itself. The camera needs only to pull back, leaving Craven to die alone on a hillside, and to pan down to the healing black flowers in the snow, mark of the planet's Gaian disdain. It is the programme's finest achievement, and perhaps its greatest political failing, that it invites this Olympian vista of cosmic history in which all tainted acts will finally be lost in a time after.

As the series draws towards its first climax in the Northmoor mines, the soundtrack increasingly emphasises gravel under wheels, shale under hiking boots, texture and tactility, as if marking with these strong evocations of discomfort the cruelty of a public world, apart from the sitting room, where suffering is an allotted human destiny. There is a shot, in near-complete darkness, of the Northmoor expedition crunching through water and shards of slate, in extreme close-up with sharply defined focal range, so each boot snaps into vision as it falls, blurring again as it lifts, as though the footfall mattered, as if to be here is harsh, surely, but at the least to be alive. A few minutes earlier, Craven's face is exhilarated, bantering with Jedburgh as they load up the Transit van that Godbolt will drive to the Northmoor entrance, alight with the pleasure of expedition. These momentary sensations – like the frequent shots of Craven holding his face or rubbing a hand, a gun or a toy across his cheek – make a direct address to the sitting room. They call for or resuscitate a specific embodiment, across the empty miles of terrestrial transmission to say, with Barthes (1980), I was here.

Between these momentary intimacies of touch and the cosmic timescale of Gaia's peaceful cure lies the public world of the series. That world operates at the narrative scale of plans, subterfuges and policies, of conspiracies, reversals, revelations and resolutions. This scale, I believe, is far closer to Kant's cosmopolitan and Euclidean space, a stage of cause-effect relations, and of the mutuality that embraces all things that exist as they exist in a single moment in time. At the same time, the series' emotional and political power derives at least in part from its refusal to move the perceptual intensities down the hierarchy of knowledges. An early sequence shows Craven going through his late daughter's things, smelling her vibrator for one last physical memory of her body. He ends that scene, distraught, her teddy bar cradled in one arm, her pistol held in his other hand, a dialectical image of the daughter he has just lost. This is a narrative image not just for the enigma it poses, nor for its allegorical evocations, but because it counterposes the tactile and narrative worlds, intimacy and action. This is the series' address to an affective politics. Rather than a sense of outraged natural justice, and more even than its anger at the desecration of nature, such scenes speak at the level of what it is to be material bodies in time and space, to inhabit rather than to act. In such a mode, gross acts of violence like the torture scenes of *24* or the visceral depictions of injuries in *C.S.I.*

Edge of Darkness: After the murder, Craven holds Gemma's teddy bear and her gun Copyright BBC.

are unneeded. The sense one has of vulnerable skin when it is cold, wet and tired is enough. This making public, this publication, of the personal and interpersonal haptic spaces belongs with what Laura U Marks (2000) describes as a cinematic memory of the senses, but which in television's residual liveness is also an address to their presence.

Colin McArthur criticises the limitations of Peter Watkins' earlier BBC drama-documentary *Culloden* and 'its central impulse . . . to give viewers the sense of actually being there at Culloden and its aftermath; its consequent impulse to make views *feel* rather than *think* history' (McArthur 1978: 48-9). Against McArthur, *Edge of Darkness* seems to argue not that the analytic mode is inappropriate to drama but that feeling, sensory participation in the screened event, is an integral part not only of an illusionistic naturalism geared towards a brainless stimulation, but that the very segregation of sense and thought is a product of a capitalist consumerism. *Edge of Darkness* offers more than a critique of this state of affairs. It offers its visual account of discomfort and vulnerability as integral to political action because they are not integral in our time – a fact underlined by Godbolt's transition from company puppet to underground activist. The depiction of public space as at least articulated with embodied space is utopian, and to that extent a political aesthetic. Emma's ghost is comforting not least because her presence is a denial of linear time. Craven's intensities of sensation are likewise denials of linear causality. The webs of intrigue that make themselves so obvious, and which mirror the obvious deceits of Thatcherite conservatism (akin to the brazen handling of the Iran-Contra scandal in the Reagan White House), convert the reciprocity of substances into a statement of the condition of a fallen polity. That sense of being there and being posthumous, with its distant echo of the phenomenological conundrum of television recording's present-absence, opens a space between the viewer and the screen. This haptic television is a lesson for future public services.

Ecology Critique

How little nature there is in *Edge of Darkness*' mise-en-scène is belied by how miraculous (the spring that starts up at the site of Emma's murder) and how eternal (the black flowers) it is. Some external shots of Craven's house and garden apart, and a brief sequence at the entrance to the mines, there are few landscape shots until the final episode. But Nature functions not only as a hypostasis of Emma's Gaia group, but as a touchstone of the third temporality in the series. Beyond the scales of the living-room's intimacies and the historical time of public affairs, there lies a secular timeframe akin to Virilio's 'landscape of events' (Virilio 1996). While this planetary or evolutionary scale is one of the attractions of the series, it is also a treacherous political terrain, not simply because it denotes the secular expropriation of a divine prerogative that Virilio fears, overseeing history from the outside, but because it separates the space of history from its making, and so destroys a grounding principle of the historical process. More specifically, the hypostasis of Nature plays directly into the hands of a cultural and political conservatism which travels in quite the opposite direction to the series' political aims.

The mutual echo of conservation with conservatism was caught not long after first transmission of the series in a polemic review by Richard Gott: 'Essentially, there are Welsh Nationalists, Scottish Nationalists, and English Greens' (Gott 1989: 31). The monocultural politics of *Edge of Darkness* brings to this conjuncture of nationalism and ecology an eco-apocalypse from the millenarian apocalyptic tradition that informed, Gott argues, the Nazi party. The national aspect of eco-conservatism is significant for the way it converges the arguments concerning public service. The original quasi-commercial license of the British Broadcasting Company founded in 1923 specified that it should operate in the 'public interest'. The Crawford Committee report of 1925, which produced the basis for the still-operative BBC Charter, designates the Corporation, then in formation, as 'the trustee for the national interest in broadcasting' (Heller 1978:13). The history of the BBC is shaped by the ongoing dialectic of public and national interest, a distinction that became brutally clear during the General Strike of 1926 and remains a chain on the Corporation's activities. Though *Edge of Darkness* surely strikes out in favour of the public, the shadow of the national is central to the series, for example in its palpable distaste for the impropriety of involving US business in UK politics, the corruption of national institutions, and in the closing scenes the distinctively English landscape of the Pennines standing as Nature.

Hans Magnus Enzensberger, in his 'Critique of Political Ecology', cites the early Marx, neatly dovetailing 'the hidden plan of nature' of Kant's universal history with the Hegelian principle of the mutuality of human desires at the basis of society:

> The *human* essence of nature exists only for *social* man; for only here does nature exist for him as a *bond* with other *men*, as his existence for others and their existence for him, as the vital element of human reality; only here does it exist as the *basis* of his own *human* existence. Only here has his *natural* existence become his *human* existence and nature become man for him. *Society* is therefore the perfected unity in essence of man and nature, the true resurrection of nature, the realized naturalism of man and the realized humanism of nature (Marx 1975: 349-50)

From an analysis of Green Party policies that tallies well with the eco-politics depicted in *Edge of Darkness*, Enzensberger argues that 'If ecology's hypotheses are valid, then capitalist societies have probably thrown away the chance of realizing Marx's project for the reconciliation of man and nature. The productive forces which bourgeois society has unleashed have been caught up with and overtaken by the destructive powers released at the same time' (Enzensberger 1988: 295). For Enzensberger, this argument leads inexorably to the eco-political duty of socialism, and the inexorable failure of an eco-politics which is not also socialist. Like Gott, he sees the Greens as wide open to fascist manipulation; unlike Gott, he also argues for the inseparability of species survival, the critique of capitalism and the global socialist project.

At an earlier moment in Enzensberger's intellectual tradition, we find Max Horkheimer arguing in 1947 that

> Since the subjugation of nature, in and outside of man, goes on without a meaningful motive, nature is not really transcended or reconciled but merely repressed. Resistance and revulsion arising from this repression of nature have beset civilization from its beginnings, in the form of social rebellions . . . as well as in the form of individual crime and mental derangement. Typical of our present era is the manipulation of this revolt by the

> prevailing forces of civilization, the use of this revolt as a means of perpetuating the very conditions by which it is stirred up and against which it is directed. Civilization as rationalized irrationality integrates the revolt of nature as a another means or instrument (Horkheimer 1992: 94)

Horkheimer gives as one instance popular Darwinism, not just the social Darwinism of 'the survival of the fittest', but the 20th century's rewriting of Kant's universal history of reason as a fruit of natural evolution. Reason is thus a product of nature, an efficient solution like hands or eyes, and ruled by nature, rather than its interpreter. At the same time, though, reason as adaptation neither abandons the pursuit of domination nor transcends the brute force of nature itself. In its apparent humility towards the natural forces that have given birth to it, instrumental reason can dismiss any understanding of nature other than as raw material for mastery. Like Enzensberger, Horkheimer distrusts any claim by the natural sciences to speak politically, especially when they pretend to reconcile, along the lines of the young Marx's project, a reconciliation of human and natural worlds.

The 'society' of which the 1844 manuscripts speak is the unrealised 'realm of freedom'. As a political thriller, *Edge of Darkness* is perfectly entitled to point to the clash between human and natural processes, and to identify nuclear technologies as a Faustian attempt at overcoming nature through her own properties that can only end disastrously. The series' judgement on the unholy matrimony of profit and power in the North Atlantic alliance hinges on the positing of nature as a counter-force, something that can be injured, but that ultimately exercises its own inhuman judgement. In its way, this Gaian hypothesis is utopian too, in that it rescues some grain of hope from the Pandora's box of nuclear waste extraction.

What seems less feasible in a political project is the reference to Christ through the later episodes, first in the figure of a statue deep in Northmoor, and most tellingly when Jedburgh enters the Temple ('Golf is a religion') of Gleneagles to offer the assembled dignitaries of the nuclear arms establishment his plutonium ingots – arms outstretched, and matched with the cross-shaped logo on the end wall. While possibly a suitably emblematic ending for Jedburgh's sacrifice of himself, the visual symbol establishes the possibility of rereading the series, from the end, as a progress through the sacraments or a sacerdotal anointing, lifting Craven and Jedburgh's tale out of the political and into the theological time and space which, in secular form, structures the Gaian vision of the conclusion. This evocation of an order obdurately removed from historical process is the opposite of the public production of dimensions. Playing on the double meaning of the word 'sens' in French, Lefebvre concludes his book with a plea for such a production

Edge of Darkness: Craven and Jedburgh share a last supper in the Northmoor bunker. Copyright BBC.

> The creation (or production) of a planet-wide space as the social foundation of a transformed everyday life open to myriad possibilities – such is the dawn beginning to break on the far horizon . . . We are concerned with what might be called a 'sense': an organ that perceives, a direction that may be conceived, and a directly lived movement progressing towards the horizon. And we are concerned with nothing that even remotely resembles a system (Lefebvre 1991: 423).

Lefebvre refers here to the 'utopians' Fourrier, Marx and Engels. In one sense at least, this a revindication, even as it is a massive rebuttal, of Kant's transcendental aesthetic and his doctrine of judgement. Kant's cosmopolitan project of universal peace demanded an *a priori* common space-time in which the species could meet and act. We now have to concede that such dimensionality does not exist, or exists only abstractly, in fragments, or as part of a contradictory ensemble in which the incommensurable space-times of environmental, political and sensory processes and of televisual narrative and domestic life fail to map onto one another. Neither reciprocal nor causal, such dimensions function to exclude, demarcate and professionalise the activities that form them, including the increasing proletarianisation of consumption, still in its earlier phases of development in the United Kingdom of 1985.

Craven is an endearingly ordinary man, but without the idealised ordinariness of Ken Loach's protagonists. He has been an unorthodox policeman in an unorthodox war, a potholer suspected of 'terrorism', a lone parent. Like Darius Jedburgh, he is ordinarily extraordinary, a character rather than a type. Compromised as his character and emotionally exhausted as Peck's performance are, he becomes capable, in tandem with Godbolt and Jedburgh, of an extraordinary act. The narrative is in this sense existential, seeking out the moment at which he will become capable of historical agency. The curiosity of this is that, by the time he moves into the heroic mode of the last episodes, one feels Craven is no longer or not merely human. The reverberations of eco-politics and theology surrounding him – his identification with trees for example – confound the psychological and phenomenological presence of the character with a historical function rather like that which Adorno ascribes to the artist: 'If the artist's work is to reach beyond his own contingency, then he must in return pay the price that, in contrast to the discursively thinking person, he cannot transcend himself and the objectively established boundaries' (Adorno 1997: 42). Unlike the philosopher, the artist must abide by the social construction of individuality and become as it were a lens through which history is drawn to a fine focus. Craven's transfiguration is of that order, as is his suffering. Even the pure accident of Emma's death is condensed from Virilio's general accident, contingency and randomness typical of modernity in general and state-sponsored violence in particular. Indeed it is the improbability of that first death that makes the rest of the story inevitable, while at the same time it makes it to some extent pointless, other than to redouble Craven's near-Buddhist sense of the world as a vale of tears. Because as random victim he can appear as both typical and unique, Craven is an exceptional vehicle through whom to address an audience both generic and cursed with individuality and the apparent randomness of a secular world. The more he becomes a cypher of communication with the audience, the shallower the psychological portrait and the more open his figure is for investment by viewers. But at the same time, his suffering is so intensely personal that the invitation is to a deeply personal engagement. A product of the relation between haptic and cosmic timescales, this is also a pointer towards a new mode of television only emergent in 1985.

In the years since *Edge of Darkness* was produced, the increasing fragmentation of television audiences and increasing competition for proletarianised attention from consumer magazines, computer games, pre-recorded media, internet and clubs, as well as the slowly fragmenting structures of work and family have made the attempt to construct a common televisual space-time increasingly problematic. In the same breath, it is important to recognise the development of what Arjun Appadurai (2002) calls 'deep democracy', broad alliances of campaign groups united geographically (Appadurai's example is

Mumbai's housing campaigns) but also translocally. The challenge of building a global public sphere is deeply problematic: is it desirable? Is it possible?. Yet it is not possible to envisage a contemporary vision for democracy that lacks an orientation, in Lefebvre's sense, towards the global, nor one that imagines a society innocent of media (in the sense that empirical social science still speaks of the 'impact' of media on society). What is to be learned from Lefebvre is not just that space must be constructed but that all dimensionality is a construct, that the processes of construction are historical and to that extent never absolute, and geographical and therefore never universal. Whatever there is of a utopian movement towards the construction of a new space-time capable of becoming public can never be systematic in the sense of an imposed structure embracing all possibilities. But it will have to be systemic, in the sense that it will have to articulate the connectivity of every disparate construction: to take into consideration the wonderful mutuality of activity in cosmopolis

Much of the debate over the Peacock report was nostalgic in tone, as though a public sphere had existed, and was about to be lost. But to some extent the public sphere has never existed, or has existed only by dint of its exclusions: the poor, women, slaves, migrants, the criminalised, and in the current context animals. The public remains an ideal form, and though our conceptions have changed since Kant, that ideal is still to a great extent what Habermas might call an unfinished project of modernity. Kant's great contribution is to have realised that discourse – philosophy for him, media for us – has the task of constituting the agora in which such a public might be able to meet. *Edge of Darkness* despite itself is politically fatalist, affectively as well as effectively conquered by its contradictory presentations of sensory and public space-times, subjugated to the secular religiosity of Gaian space-time. Yet nonetheless the series can serve as an inspiration for the task of building dimensions in which a public sphere with some kind of global orientation might be possible. Television may even benefit from its fragmentation, where the political movements of most consequence often appear to be those with the most intensely local perceptions of their causes, micro-publics of agency rather than consumption.

The attempt to build a public sphere, even in the immanently global terms of eco-politics, will always be tainted with the history of nationalism, unless and until the dimensions of the public sphere extend to an appreciation that on global scales it cannot be other than mediated. Grounding work on televisual time (Williams 1974, Feuer 1983, White 1986, Dienst 1995) and space (Spigel 1992, Hartley 1992, Weber 1996, McArthy 2001), with their analyses of the segmentation and realisation of flow and the locations and constructions of domestic and public space, provide the bases for a movement beyond the terms of the bourgeois public sphere and the modern nation. McArthy especially is adamant that the term 'public' can today no longer be reserved for a civil society unassailed by commerce. Citizenship, and with it public space, is grounded in the trade in audiences. Yet this traffic is not without internal contradictions that point towards towards the capabilities of the intricated networks of electronic media, now far more rarely discrete from one another, in complex local spaces where digital, telecom and broadcast operate in consort and in conflict, and in ever more deranged global labyrinths of interconnection and risk. The politics of trade, as *Edge of Darkness* makes so clear, is also the trade in politicians. Political science rightly quizzes the possibility and desirability of global governance (for example Rosenau 1990, 2003, and the contributors to Held and McGrew 2000). What earlier traditions called 'culture', 'society' and 'politics', is, in the 21st century, none of these, which have become abstractions, but media: the material mediations of the connectivities that constitute humanity as polis, and that articulate the polis with techne and physis. If it is desirable or possible to build translocal public dimensions, expanded beyond the narrow confines and imagined community of the national public, then there are only media with which to build them. The rich interplay of space-times in *Edge of Darkness* indicate some of their possibilities, even if it does so only negatively, in the failure to build a public space capable of surviving the onslaught of Thatcherism and Reaganomics.

Bare Life

Craven is no coward, despite his name, but he is defeated. Destitute of all his loves, he has withdrawn from the polis, suffers its buffets like a leaf in a storm. The perpetual evocations of touch in the way he is filmed even more than his predilection for long silences and barely muttered speech suggest he is untying his bonds with the society he has served, not so much becoming animal as diminishing his humanity. There is less and less of a shell protecting him from natural forces, from rain, cold, bruises. The veneer of norms and the perpetual round of half-meant greetings that stitch humanity together and shield us from the cold are peeling away. In a more optimistic or a spiritual perspective, he might well be on the road to revelation, to surrender to the merely sensuous experience of his world. But always, right through to the final *dénouement*, Craven is open not to wonder but to pain. He suffers, not only in himself, but in suffering the slings and arrows of his outrageous fortune. He suffers but does not instigate the plot, save only in asking 'Why?': a question his bare existence would be sufficient to pose. And yet even that question is mumbled and muted: he does not ask why God wills it so, but which instruments He used to bring about catastrophe. Like Kafka's K, he does not question the violence of the world, but nonetheless doggedly demands to know the processes through which it is carried out. Not only does he not seek vengeance: he does not expect justice, or any moral outcome; only that there be some order to the machinery that has delivered him outside the boundaries of the law. The black flowers offer some kind of resolution: their adaptation to a colder, darker world adumbrates Gaia's survival, even if the humans hang themselves. But a resolution is not an answer. Craven's questioning, his insistence that there should be some significant structure left whose authority is adequate to explain his own exclusion from it, is the most powerful political question of the series. It concerns what is left of a man who finds himself outside, alone on the moors in the rain neither hunted nor searched for, excluded.

The Scottish artist Ian Hamilton Finlay struck a medallion with, on one side, two classical pillars and the word 'Justice'. On the other, the same two pillars support the blade of a guillotine with the motto 'Terror'. The equation expresses the revolutionary moment of any new legal system, the threat of violence which belongs, in Benjamin's (1979a) phrase, to 'constituting violence', the extra-legal wielding of force that establishes any legality. This violent accession to the monopoly of violence in legal systems establishes a bounded state, a territory within which the law holds good. It is at the boundaries, both geographical and metaphysical, that violence is deployed in its 'constituting' form: in the banishment of the outlaw, for example, who is in that action removed from membership of the legal community, deprived of rights, to become fair game for any hunter. Giorgio Agamben, in his work on sovereignty, argues that the status of the outcast whom it is permitted to kill but not to sacrifice – that is, who may not be part of any ritual, including ritual execution, because they have forfeit their political being – is the same as that of the sovereign, in the sense that both are outside the law, or rather perched in a boundary between inclusion and an exclusion which nonetheless has the force of law and is therefore to that extent included as exclusion.

In *The Accursed Share* (1988) Georges Bataille, renegade surrealist, grounds the concept of sovereignty in unrestrained expenditure. Bataille's sovereign must give, extravagantly and even mercilessly, on the model of the sun's endless giving of light and heat. Commenting on Bataille in the context of his critique of modernity, Jürgen Habermas argues that this formulation pitches the domain of the sacred outwith the boundaries of legal as well as rational discourse, in a binary opposition that permits of no dialectical interplay:

> If sovereignty and its source, the sacred, are related to the world of purposive-rational action in an absolutely heterogeneous fashion, if the subject and reason are constituted only by excluding all kinds of sacred power, if the other of reason is more than just the irrational or the unknown – namely, the *incommensurable*, which cannot be touched by reason except at the cost of an explosion of the rational subject – then there is no possibility of a theory that reaches beyond the horizon of what is accessible to

> reason and thematizes, let alone analyzes, the interaction of reason with a transcendent source of power (Habermas 1987: 235-6).

Agamben's extension of Bataille's argument responds indirectly to this criticism by investigating the figure of the Roman *homo sacer*, the outcast stripped of all bonds with the polis, a bare life, who nonetheless is included in a system that names him as outcast: the outlaw defined by law. 'Man, for millennia, remained what he was for Aristotle: a living animal also capable of a political existence; modern man is an animal in whose politics the life of the living creature is in question' (Foucault 1976: 188). Citing approvingly this line of Foucault, Agamben argues that 'Not simple natural life, but life exposed to death (bare life or sacred life) is the originary political element' (Agamben 1998: 88) in an order whose terminals are symmetrical: 'the sovereign is the one with respect to whom all men are potentially *homines sacri*, and *homo sacer* is the one with respect to whom all men act as sovereigns' (Agamben 1998: 84). Ancient and feudal orders maintained this originating sacred violence; but in the modern state, it has dissolved into 'constituted violence', the banality of everyday law, and in the extreme case into the routine violence of the concentration camp. Since then, Agamben argues, the biological body and the political animal have become indistinguishable in a brutal biopolitics of fear and the constant threat of violence in a polis which now no longer has the sacred for a boundary.

Critics of contemporary ecopolitics like Blühdorn (2000) and Barry (1999) argue that the hypostasis of nature as entirely external to the polis is a significant weakness that leaves Green parties with no purchase inside the polis on popular desires and popular motives. Placing such arguments alongside Agamben's would seem to imply that making policy dependent on a sacred domain utterly outside the polis leaves the polis prey to an indeterminate and endemic violence while, ironically, stripping nature of one of its greatest powers, mortality. Most of all, the removal of the sacred from the boundary where it was simultaneously inside and outside the polis desanctifies human life. Deep ecology pursues the logic Leo Marx (1964: 301) identifies in *Moby Dick*, 'a culture that would deify the Nature it is engaged in plundering', to the point at which it is the polis that is plundered in the name of nature. Such is the condition that produces terrorism, at least where terror is a mode of politics where, in place of communication, violence mediates a sacred demand to an audience deemed incapable of hearing it. Of course, faith in Gaia no more makes an ecoteur a terrorist than faith in Allah or Jehovah. The irony of *Edge of Darkness* is that it is not the suspected terrorist Gemma who turns out to be the instrument of nature's imagined wrath, but the CIA spook Jedburgh, whose death has all the hallmarks of the sacrifice, since his suicidal assassination of the assembled arms dealers and generals is accomplished in the name of absolute justification derived from beyond human affairs. Craven, meanwhile, completes his withdrawal, an action which should make him the unique *homo sacer* and allow him to escape into nature. Instead, however, Craven becomes almost the archetype of the biopolitical subject, left to die on the hillside by a legitimate sovereignty which no longer regards him.

The poles represented by Jedburgh and Craven in the final episode denote two feasible strategies for deep ecology: withdrawal from the polis and assault on its imaginary core. But as Eco argued so cogently in the time of the Brigate Rosse, terrorism 'doesn't weaken the system, but rather recreates the consensus around the symbolic ghost of its "heart", wounded and outraged' (Eco 1988: 175). Every attack on its absent heart is additional evidence that the political system possesses one, but in an age of networks, discourses and institutions, there is no heart at all. By acting as if there were, the terrorist helps reproduce the lie that the state is the source of power. At the same time, acting in the name of a sacred nature, the ecoterrorist does not act against the polis, but precisely in the same way as it: by reducing its members to bare lives, whose deaths are not sacrifices but mere fatalities, messages sent to an absent sovereign whose rule the terrorist maintains in the worst faith by pretending that there exists a decision-making entity other than that in whose name he acts. Jedburgh is sending a message encoded in dead people whose status he disdains but which nonetheless he appends to his message as if it did matter. Bad faith.

Craven seems at first glance the more honest man, turning his back on police, hospital, prison, to go and die under the rain. As a psychological portrait wholly credible: Craven is Frodo lost in the shadow realm, object of a mortal gaze that both identifies and disdains him utterly. But this is an entirely individual salvation, and as such not a political act at all. The reverse of the ban that includes what it excludes, Craven's withdrawal excludes the polis from the living creature, the life from his own living (this is after all a suicidal act), and in the long shot of his distant figure, excludes too the televisual apparatus and its audiences. In that last twist, the resolution of the narrative is also a withdrawal from public space. It is this felt impossibility of the character and ultimately the story to reconnect to the polis that both reveals the polis for its tawdry self and establishes Craven's end as tragedy. It is as though he has mistaken his fate for destiny, and in giving all sovereignty to nature, has abandoned all freedom, all agency for himself. So finally Craven adds to Jedburgh's knowing address to an absent hierarchy his withdrawal from the polis as a model for politics, and his silence for public debate. A brilliant, tragic depiction of the impossibility of a public debate on ecological issues, the series leaves us with one of the more profound questions of popular mediations of environmentalism: what kind of creature is a human?

Are We Not Men?

X-men, X-2 and Genetic Modification

All serv'd, all seving! nothing stands alone;
The chain holds on, and where it ends, unknown
Alexander Pope, *Essay on Man*, Ep. III, 25-6

Mutant Identity

Missing from the current account are films like *The Fast and the Furious*, films where the wanton annihilation of natural resources is celebrated, consumerism is triumphant, the green world only a backdrop to blacktop, and the highest virtues – solidarity, brotherhood, liberty – enacted in rituals of guiltless destruction. On Agamben's principle of inclusive exclusion, almost all big-budget films are ecologically-themed in the sense that they deploy landscapes as location and animals as props, or alternatively because they meticulously exclude them. Not only is the ecological footprint of film production, distribution and exhibition immense (a point I am indebted to Dean Ballinger for bringing to my attention) and as completely erased from the finished product as possible, but films are to a great extent dependent on such residual and hard-to-avoid natural properties as human bodies and sunlight. Nonetheless, the typical blockbuster is ecological in the more or less meticulous reduction of the green world to backgrounds, the prevalence of urban settings, ubiquitous cars, helicopters, aircraft and speedboats. Certainly the *X-men* movies and the rest of the Marvel franchise – *Hulk*, *Spiderman*, *Daredevil* – enjoy their share of gas-guzzling and wreckage. But they also voice a complex take on mutation and modification, the internal turmoil of *homo superior* in the face of what Neil Evernden (1992: 120) calls 'the domestication of the gene'.

In the spring of 2003, leaders of the Human Genome Project announced that their task was complete: they had secured a basic map of human inheritance. The human body has about 100 trillion cells. In the nucleus of the vast majority are two copies of the genome, one from each parent. Each genome has between 60 and 80,000 genes arranged in 23 chromosomes, the whole genome containing a billion codons each comprising three molecules selected from a list of four: adenine, cytosine, guanine and thymine. To build a body, these genomes have to be copied and recopied over and over again. In the process, as a result of internal copy errors or environmental factors, changes occur: mutations (Ridley 1999). The genome is deeply conservative and tries to repair changes, but some get through. Sometimes these are useful genes, coding for resistance to malaria for example, and get handed on to the next generation. Some are destructive; but if, like Alzheimer's, they strike after the age of childbearing, the chances are that they will get passed on too. As these examples suggest, minute differences between the DNA of individuals can be deeply significant, even though the vast majority of the genome is identical for everyone: differences large enough to provide forensic scientists with genetic 'fingerprints' and the US Administration with biometric passports. Significant enough to indicate that *the* map of the human genome is a generalisation abstracted from diversity.

Much knowledge of the genome is patented, owned by corporations, and many of the techniques used to gain such knowledge are also used in genetic engineering, the modification of genes to produce medically or commercially desirable mutations. The first experiments were conducted in 1972; in 1974 a moratorium was announced; at the 1975 Asilomar conference, safety standards were agreed and experiments resumed. Gene therapy for human illness has yet to achieve stunning success, but remains an uncontroversial alternative or supplement to conventional medical treatments. Modification of plant genes began in 1983. By 1996 the process was widespread in food crops in the USA. In 1999, however, Monsanto introduced crops genetically resistant to its otherwise indiscriminate herbicide Roundup to a Europe still reeling from the mishandling of the BSE epidemic. Genetic modification became a major political issue for environmental activists and Green parties, who had achieved the peak of their popular success in the 1998 European Parliament elections. Since 1988, it has been possible to splice new genes into animal embryos, producing, for example, sheep whose milk contains human clotting factor, used to treat haemophilia. In a parallel development, attempts have been made to increase the meat and dairy yield of food animals by genetic modification. Again, entrance into the food chain has proved the political sticking point. But many protesters also finger the dangers of engineered genes reaching wild populations, and others raise ethical issues concerning the morality of intervening in natural processes. At least one general election – in Aotearoa New Zealand in 2001 – has been fought on the issue, in this case also raising the sacred stewardship of the land among first peoples against the industrialisation of farming methods. A world-wide boom in demand for organic products is very probably linked with the increasing public unease with the commercial development of genetic engineering.

Which is the moment at which Bryan Singer's screen adaptation of Marvel Comics' *X-men* is released. 'Every few hundred millennia, evolution leaps forward' intones Professor Xavier over the title sequence of the first film. We are in a near future where spontaneous mutations in the human population produce a generation gifted with idiosyncratic superpowers – the ability to control fire, heat, storms; to heal instantly, to teleport objects, to walk through walls. The drama of both films derives from a three-sided struggle. Professor Xavier provides a haven for mutants and strives for coexistence with humans. Ordinary humans threaten the mutants with imprisonment and violence, both legal and spontaneous. And Magneto, also a mutant, seeks to spark all-out war between humans and mutants with the goal of mutant victory. Magneto's backstory opens the film: in a Nazi camp, ripped away from his parents who wear yellow stars, he discovers his ability to control magnetism and metals. The theme of the Shoah recurs throughout the film as a bedrock on which to develop its message of tolerance. Magneto, laying out his case, places mutants in the position of the Polish Jews of the opening sequence when he speaks of them being assaulted 'simply because they were born different from those in power '. The web of inclusion/exclusion is extended further when he adds that the struggle for mutant supremacy will be waged 'by any means necessary', a phrase inextricably associated with Malcolm X and the Black Power movement. That these echoes of the Holocaust and the civil rights movement are not restricted to Magneto is clear from Xavier's horror at realising that Wolverine is the victim of 'experimentation on mutants', an echo of Mengele's 'genetic' experiments of 1943-4 at Auschwitz-Birkenau, recaptured in the costuming and prosthetic make-up for another victim of experimentation, the telepath Victor, in *X-2*.

The long shadow of Nazi eugenics has lain across genetic science for half a century, bolstered by occasional memorials to the eugenic sterilisation programmes of otherwise model liberal democracies like the Scandinavian countries (Broberg and Roll-Hansen 1996) and the 'lost generation' of Australian Aborigines. Equally 'positive' eugenics' aim of producing improved babies seems ludicrous when painted in the colours of Hitler's Lebensborn project to encourage 'Aryan' foetuses, but the same thought is clear in selective immigration policies, apartheid, Jim Crow laws and contemporary European fascist parties. That bizarre invention of the Southern states, 'miscegenation', is still problematic for any Hollywood film that expects major box-office returns: *X-men*'s only African-American character, Storm (Halle Berry) hints at a romantic attachment to Night Crawler, but he is in thrall to his religious mania and it can be safely presumed he will never act on his impulses. Gene science requires all the help it can get to wriggle out from under the shadow of eugenics, and to claim that its revindication of bloodlines is not the required excuse for mass sterilisation programmes.

Genetic fingerprinting is a less fraught issue, but nonetheless it too has it place in *X-men*. The first film's initiating action is the proposal of a law all mutants to be officially registered. (The irony is of course that just such a law is now being enacted in the USA, biometrics allying with homeland security to produce a bio-security operated against the cosmopolitan). Again, the shadow of the Shoah hangs over the way this law is presented. Registration, surveillance, pathologisation, marginalisation and stripping of rights have all too often followed one another. Genetic screening has become a major issue in the USA in recent years, not least because of the targeting of African Americans in a bid to curtail the incidence of sickle-cell anaemia, a genetic disorder relatively common in people of West African descent, but also among many Mediterranean hereditary gene lines.

In the State of Virginia, which 'continued to sterilise the mentally handicapped into the 1970s' (Ridley 1999: 290), 'newborn screening is mandatory for all screened disorders *except* sickle cell which is voluntary' (Duster 2003: 52). Fears of genetic profiling include its use by insurers to set premiums, by government to identify citizens for surveillance, by immigration authorities to police the flow of people (Appadurai's [1996] 'ethnoscapes'), and by health services to control the progenerative choices of specific populations, but the Virginia example suggests also an ideological link between sterilisation and gene counselling, where pregnant women may be confronted with the possibility of terminating a pregnancy on the basis of genetic screening, effectively achieving the goal of the sterilisation programme by other means. In particular, the categorisation of genetic screening results in categories that enshrine race and ethnicity is especially strong in the USA (such categorisation is relatively unknown in the European Union). The Nuremberg trials were explicit in condemning 'the specification of ethnic and racial groups in legislation by the state' (Duster 2003: 40). But since the USA has a history of social stratification by race and ethnicity, the categories have become naturalised to the extent that, despite all sociological and scientific evidence to the contrary, gathering data on a racialised basis is enshrined in medical practice, and therefore rarely questioned when applied in mandatory screening programmes.

The Council of Europe's Convention on Human Rights and Biomedicine, Article 11, states: 'Any form of discrimination against a person on grounds of his or her genetic heritage is prohibited' (1997). Likewise UNESCO's Universal Declaration on the Human Genome and Human Rights declares in its Article 6 'No one shall be subjected to discrimination based on genetic characteristics that is intended to infringe or has the effect of infringing human rights, fundamental freedoms and human dignity' (1997). Both documents refer to the UN's 1948 Universal Declaration of Human Rights with its resounding assertion of 'the inherent dignity and of the equal and inalienable rights of all members of the human family'. Stan Lee and Jack Kirby's *X-Men* comics clearly share this commitment to racial equality, an issue Lee addresses in interviews, angrily recalling the anti-Semitism and racism aimed at African and Hispanic Americans during his post-war youth. In at least the case of Victor, the mutant son of the rogue militarist Stryker,

X-2: Professor Xavier's X-Men as victims of suspicion and fear. Courtesy BFI Stills.

there is also an echo of the abuse of the disabled, whose campaigns for civil and human rights have marked the last few decades. yet who stand in some respects as markers for the eugenicist tendency in genetic medicine.

As Kerr and Shakespeare note, (2002: 127), rather unjustly including all medical professionals,

> They have been trained to think of illness and impairment as a problem that must be solved through medical intervention. If a condition cannot be cured, it is not illogical for them to think that it should be prevented. Yet in the case of congenital impairments, this means removing the person, not just removing the disease.

Though eugenic sterilisation is less acceptable today than it was even in the 1980s in the UK when the House of Lords refused a young woman with Down's syndrome the right to marry, there is often still prenatal counselling for prospective parents that sways against bearing children with disabilities, and still social and employment prejudice against people with disabilities, and to some extent towards their parents and siblings. To the more visible disabilities, genetic screening adds the possibility of lifelong, specific attention paid by surveillant health and welfare services. The attention makes people with disabilities in many respects 'less equal' than their peers. The 'Mutant Registration

Act' of *X-men* is then more than a random plot device. But this is after all a popcorn movie, based on a successful comics franchise with a substantial fan base, blessed with potential for toys, games, collectibles. If it is to be a lesson in civics, it must also undertake to be a popular media artefact first and foremost.

Bioethics, Biopolitics

To evoke once more the world of *Whale Rider*, Paikea's destiny involves overcoming her fate: the biological fate of being born female, and the traditional fate that debars her from leadership. But this is produced neither by 'coming of age' nor by an act of will. It is orchestrated through the the calling of the ancestors, the whales, an action fraught with peril. Tradition appears as the recurrence of patterns, but also as the ongoing chain of births, past and future, that link generations past to the present and the future. Likewise, the tradition of *Whale Rider* is a fund of stories that speak to the present about how actions should be conducted. In some ways, technology may be seen as the tradition of Europeans. In Marx's terms, machines are ossifications of dead labour, the skills and knowledges of generations of workers abstracted and realised in a device. But Europeans' technologies differ from tradition in that they are anonymous, both in the sense that they abstract skills from persons, and in the sense that Giedion has of technologies like baking, knitting and plumbing as anonymous formations of history (Giedion 1948; I am grateful to Ian Stuart for clarifying these ideas). Nonetheless, even science recognises the presence of the past:

> I am not speaking of randomness . . . , but of the central principle of all history – *contingency*. A historical explanation does not rest on direct deductions from the laws of nature , but on an unpredictable sequence of antecedent states, where any major change in any step of the sequence would have altered the final result. This final result is therefore dependent, or contingent, upon everything that came before – the unerasable and determining signature of history (Gould 1989: 283).

Though Gould is speaking specifically of biological inheritance, his words reverberate with Marx's observation that we do not make history under conditions of our own choosing, and that the accumulated weight of the past guides, structures and constrains what pretensions to freedom we may retain. If ecology has taught us anything, it is that not only the past but the whole of our environment shapes and structures what it is to be alive and to act. Noting that technologies are the embodiment of past generations' skills just as the present environment is the product of aeons of evolution has significant implications for the concept of human freedom. What is peculiar about the Western approach to these constraints is their anonymity.

Whakapapa, the ongoing lineage that binds a people and a land together in Maori cosmology, is a personalised understanding of what Europe understands by genes. It would be unusual to find a health policy counselling the memorisation of your family tree; but some are already recommending keeping a copy of your DNA handy, like a barcode, to check with potential partners whether any potential offspring might be at risk of genetic disorders. And of course, there is the positive eugenic aspect of genetic medicine: the potential to select desirable genes to be spliced into your embryonic offspring. Paikea's recognition of her destiny, to cite Marx again, is the effort to make history, despite fate, despite the fact that we must make history under conditions that we have not chosen. The European techno-scientific response is to change fate. If, to amend Freud, biology is fate, then biology must be remade, instrumentalised. For traditional society, that is dangerous not simply because it insults the ancestral voices that sing through the bloodlines, but because it is a change that is then fated to be handed on down the line into future generations. Far from opening up possibilities, by altering the present in such a definitive way, genetic science threatens to close down options for the future by predetermining them. And to the extent that they are dependent on our present, the future is restricted from being what by definition it should be: other than the present.

In a series of lectures published under the title 'The Future of Human Nature', Jürgen Habermas opens a discussion of the ethical implications of bioscience and genetic medicine by referring to debates on abortion. For some, the embryo is an agglomeration of cells; for others it is already imbued with rights. In the latter belief, the mere fact that these cells are imprinted with their parental DNA and therefore biologically determined makes them human. At this juncture Habermas pauses to assert the difference between the possession of rights and the ethical obligation for humans not to interfere with or terminate the cells. Human rights, he argues, are not the possessions of individuals, in the way eye colour or height are. Instead, they derive exclusively from 'interpersonal relations of mutual respect' (Habermas 2003: 33). The very idea, the very experience, of selfhood is a product of communicative communities in which the individual comes to have a place. And free will, far from being an innate gift of God, is 'a precarious achievement of finite beings who may attain something like "strength," if at all, only if they are mindful of their physical vulnerability and social dependence' (Habermas 2003: 34). Within a communicative system, a moral right is absolute to the extent that it is a necessary attribute of any member of the system – in a global age, a system that, for Habermas, encompasses all human beings. An ethical value, on the other hand, can be discussed, debated, weighed up for good or ill.

In most societies, the moral takes precedence over the ethical: rights over 'goods'. But when there is a breech in the conditions on which the right is premised – for example the self-determination of individual humans – then ethical debate has to take on an unaccustomed precedence. Today, instead of adjusting ourselves to natural processes, we have broken down the differentiation between human and natural (and incidentally between theory and practice, at least in the life sciences). In addition to mastering the natural environment, technoscience now seems capable of mastering human nature. Habermas raises the question of whether, in this process, the person so generated is both capable of an autonomous life and able to meet as an equal with others in her communicative community. Put slightly differently, how do we balance the rights of parents to alter the genetic make-up of their children with the rights of the children themselves, or more specifically, how can this be a moral relationship when it is asymmetrical: the designed cannot argue her design with her designer? Perhaps most damning of all, Habermas asks 'why – if biotechnology is subtly undermining our identity as members of the species – should we *want* to be moral?' (Habermas 2003: 73).

Habermas is clear that human rights and the human ethics that depend upon them are species-specific, in that we recognise the equality of other humans. In distinguishing morals and ethics from mere feelings of disgust, he separates the communicative community as species from the continuities of physis. But the contrary seems to be at stake, at least in the movies. The title sequence of Ang Lee's *Hulk* observes the genetic scientist at work, hypodermically extracting bioluminescence from a jellyfish, severing a starfish limb, electrocuting a sea-cucumber, slicing a lizard with a scalpel and finally gassing a rhesus monkey. Every audience seems to wince, even at the assault on the jellyfish; evidence of a capacity for trans-species identifications. Our morality may be based on other communicative regimes than the verbal, other empathies than those grounded in a shared species identity, and on non-linear, systemic polylogues. Curiously the prospect that his self-induced mutation has been handed on to his unsuspecting son, the infant Hulk, seems to induce less squeamishness, which might suggest that it is the *perception* of harm that evokes identification, and perhaps supports Habermas' argument that rational discourse is the basis of human communication, rather than emotional bonds. The inference of Habermas' arguments is that our emotional empathy with virtual animals may not extend to the instrumentalist abuse of real ones, just as our generalised and sentimental attachment to conservation rarely extends to abandoning the internal combustion engine. What is at stake is an ethics that does not assume the universality of the moral, and we might add is not restricted to a single species presumed to be distinguished by its reason and its speech. Classical economics presupposes a rational and perfectly informed purchaser, parallel to Habermas's ideally rational and equal interlocutor. The problem is that consumption is neither rational nor perfectly informed. Like the economic, the political is concerned with the good life, and decreasingly if at all with universal morals. When universal right can no longer be presumed, ethics, bioethics in particular, become politics.

In a postscript contesting some objections to his theses and questions, Habermas clarifies what is at stake here. The central issue is the risk that individual autonomy, and therefore the premise of morality, might be undone by the reification and instrumentalisation of human life at the embryonic stage before it can make choices. The moral self-understanding of individuals is the precondition for ethical debate, but if that self-understanding is undermined, then ethical discussion cannot take place in the freedom and equality of dialogue: 'No arguments from the moral language game itself can be mustered against a eugenic self-instrumentalization of the human species which changes the very rules of the game' (Habermas 2003: 92). At risk in the development of embryonic stem cell research and the possibility of a genetic supermarket for designer babies is the very possibility of a moral universe.

In the course of his argument, Habermas (2003: 59) cites Hannah Arendt in terms that suggest what he believes might come after the ethical. Arendt writes of the principle of natality:

> the new beginning inherent in birth can make itself felt in the world only because the newcomer possesses the capacity of beginning something anew, that is, of acting. In this sense of initiative, an element of action, and therefore of natality, is inherent in all human activities. Moreover, since action is the political activity par excellence, natality, and not mortality, may be the central category of political, as distinguished from metaphysical, thought (Arendt 1958: 9)

Presuming, if we dare, that there is no gene for immortality, everyone dies. In Heidegger, the being-towards-death occupies a central position in the meaning of humanity as that sole species that is aware of its own mortality. Arendt's argument is more inclusive: everyone is also born, and the neonate is endowed with a special privilege, a shadow of Benjamin's 'weak messianic power'. For Benjamin, every generation has among its tasks the work of judging the past, since past generations looked to posterity for judgement, and we are that posterity – at any given moment, we are the only ones, of all the people who have ever lived, who are alive today. But the infant has a further role. With every birth, a new start is made. Like the longed-for messiah, every infant bears the possibility of some unthought-of future capability. For Arendt that capacity lives on in the capacity for political action. But if the infant's biological fate has been designed rather than accidental, what initiative, what power to initiate, has been rent from them? Can the capacity to instigate futurity be bred out of the individual, or indeed the species? And if so, are we faced with a changing mode of politics, from the realm of action which Arendt isolates, to a realm of sovereignty and the exercise of power; from a rational and moral polis to one constituted with neither? Have global and national governance moved beyond the scale at which dialogue was possible, entering an era of multiple interlocking polylogues between institutions?

Systems

In May 2004, Monsanto announced that it was abandoning plans for genetically modified ('Roundup Ready') wheat, claiming that the move was 'a business decision'. Consumer lobby groups claimed victory, but the opposition of the Canadian Wheat Board, the world's largest wheat and barley marketing agency, was probably more significant. That in turn was grounded on the regulatory bodies of major overseas markets in the United Kingdom and Japan who demanded the separation of modified and conventional supplies, something current technology cannot deliver. And they in turn, it seems probable, have been persuaded by consumer resistance to GM foods and demands for clear labelling (Flavelle 2004). Monsanto, meanwhile, reassured their investors by emphasising that corn, canola and cotton modifications will continue to be marketed, and that GM wheat will be back on the shelves once the technology for distinguishing it from conventional cereals is in place.

This story suggests several versions of a political narrative. Firstly, there is a narrative of the successful self-regulation of an industry. Then there is the market imperative story: the free market legislates itself without the need for state intervention. There is the triumph of consumer pressure narrative. And there is a narrative of the corporation itself as no longer a free agent but caught between the competing pressures of its largest customer and its investors (other probable pressures will include factors such as the competition to develop GM crops before another company patents them). Unaccounted for in any of these stories is the anomalous acceptance of other GM crops, including foodstuffs like corn and canola. The role of the state in these narratives is marked by only two national governments of wealthy and powerful trading nations (each of which may also have interests in promoting their own genetic projects at the expense of Monsanto). Smaller nations may well be vulnerable to commercial pressures, forced to weigh up the costs and benefits of lowering barriers to GM crops against the potential for developing exports and creating wealth.

Such interconnected series of modifiers to political decision making parallel the ecological system into which GM plants are introduced. Certainly there are worries about the effects of GM food on present and future generations. Equally disturbing is the fear that herbicide-resistant strains either supplant indigenous strains by out-competing them in the environment of industrial farming, or fail to supply ecological benefits that conventional plants do, for example providing a niche for insects which, while they may be pests for one species, are beneficial to another, perhaps in a different phase of their life cycle, a return to Rachel Carson's *Silent Spring*. These fears may sometimes refer to metaphysical absolutes outside the reach of reason – to God or gods – but most share alertness to the interconnected nature of action. Habermas' theory of communicative rationality breaks down at this juncture, where the connections are potentially chaotic cascades of diffuse interactions, rather than organisations of linear causality. Where it rejoins his argument, however, is in what Robert Hunter (2002) refers to as 'the dread response', which he has identified in nuclear as well as genetic technology: the public dread of technologies whose consequences are not so much unknown as unpredictable – belonging to a future which they may do too much to damage and constrain. Unlike, for example, the people whose DNA profiles may well be used to control their movements, the movement of genetically modified crops is presented by their corporate manufacturers as requiring no regulation and no barriers. Free movement of humans is clearly seen as entropic, while the movement of genes is presented as homeostatic. Yet the opposite case is easily made: human migration is an emergent behaviour, while the propagation of modified genes is entropic, in the sense that it reduces the quantum of difference in the global system.

In the comics, developed in the nuclear rather than the genetic era, mutation is a randomising moment in the world, something that marks it off as a modern, and in Beck's (1995) sense a risk society. Hulk is exposed to gamma radiation, Spiderman to the bite of a radioactive arachnid. In the X-men films, the voiceover admonition that 'every few hundred millennia, nature leaps forward' suggest that the mutation is only evolution, albeit a startlingly new form of evolution. Xavier asks, at the beginning of the second film, 'are mutants the next link in the evolutionary chain or simply a new species of humanity fighting for their share of the world?' The ambiguous categories – are the X-men mutants human or not? – establish a quandary for the UNESCO and Council of Europe imperatives, which are founded on 'the equal and inalienable rights of all members of the human family'. If a new species, then mutants have no share in that family, and therefore no recognisable rights. In effect, they have only the rights of animals, in which case they may be represented but cannot represent themselves in a declaration of *human* rights. On the other hand, a new species may also have new obligations, which Xavier stands for: obligations and duties *vis-à-vis* the older humanity. But in the near-future of the films, Magneto's antipathy to humanity would appear to be without such duties.

What is missing from Habermas' account of supermarket eugenics is precisely what Magneto makes manifest: that moment of exile which Flusser so urgently wants to surpass, the moment of exception, of Nietzschean aristocracy; the moment of class. The further fear articulated by the films is not that mutation will close down the future. To that extent, the films can be considered apologia for genetic modification. Instead, it is that only some will be invited to join the future, and that by accident of birth, one of the categories of discrimination that is explicitly condemned in the UN Declaration. Instead of the genetically-determined risking becoming slaves, it is *homo sapiens* who risk becoming the servants of *homo superio*r. The reversal imitates the tales of settler cultures, in which the genocide of the American Indians for example is told as a tale of rape, destruction and massacre of the whites by the first people. It also echoes the same fear that treats the migrant as alien and that is articulated in the upside down demagogic ideologies blaming the poor and oppressed for 'taking our jobs'. The connection between migration and mutation recurs in the sense of unease both evoke, an anxiety now resonating with fears of weaponised viruses and more general fear of pandemics like SARS. The nuclear threat has been replaced, in the popular mediations of Hollywood, with a generalised fear of the biosphere. The long-repressed spectre of racism and eugenics has returned to popular memory as the troubled and troubling mutant species *homo superior*. Just when it seemed that race had lost its biological determinacy in favour of a cultural neo-racism (Balibar 1991), the new life sciences and the new bio-panics have dragged the meanings of the otherwise meaningless – as earlier skin pigment so now the arrangement of nucleotides – back to the centre stage of nationalism and fundamentalism.

The recruitment of genetic science to the cause of homeland security is a snapshot moment of a disturbing attempt to restore a universalist moral basis to the emergent risk society. President Bush Jnr's embrace of Christian fundamentalism, like the religious fundamentalisms of increasing influence in Israel and Islam, have attempted to bring what Luhmann (1989) calls the functionally differentiated systems that compose society – law, politics, economy, science, media – into a single system. Any government's first power base lies in legislation, as in various right-wing attempts to legislate a narrow definition of family. But through control of subsidies, it may also attempt to regulate other areas. For instance, according to the Waxman Report,

> Federal agencies with global reputations for scientific excellence depend upon the objective input of leading scientists and the impartial analysis of scientific evidence to develop effective policies. The Bush Administration, however, has repeatedly suppressed, distorted, or obstructed science to suit political and ideological goals' (House of Representatives 2003: 32).

Like the Taliban, the Bush administration seeks a return to values it believes once held sway, and to encourage and in some instances to enforce a moral core to the whole of society's activities. Doing so requires abandoning both reason and debate in favour of an assertion of faith. It gives rise to an increasingly fearful system, in which risks that do not square with the ideology are minimised, and imaginary dangers that do fit are treated as imminent disasters. Such unification of society implies increasing fortification of boundaries against alien influences, and an increasing devotion to homogeneity. The danger is not so much that such homeostatic yearnings stop desirable changes as that by excluding change and embracing stasis, they open the doors to entropy. Green politics that embrace conservation of what exists in place of evolution run similar risks.

Evolution

A core theme of this book, the uses of technology to mediate between the human and the natural, becomes disquieting in real-world genetic modification. In communicative uses, such technologies mediate between the human and the natural, making visible processes that otherwise might be impossible to photograph, from storms to the deep ocean, beached whales to a revolt against battery farming. In depictions of an order of nature which otherwise does not exist, a different relationship begins to form. In the first thirty minutes of Ang Lee's *Hulk*, for example, there is a palpable sense of the unholy or at the least the *unheimlich*, the uncanny. As feminist critics have argued at least since Gena Corea's 1986 book, there is a kind of masculinist hubris involved in interventions into reproductive technologies which we experience as disturbing, even disgusting. Such disgust concerns the crossing of boundaries, such fundamental boundaries as the outside and the inside - an effect constantly used in horror films, where the wetness of entrails disfigures the skins of monsters. Fans describe their fascination with such images, but likewise the repulsion. The monstrous is always paradoxical: inside-out, sacred and vile, unspeakable yet speaking. But the paradoxes are curiously static. The stories have to end with the restoration of the known, or in the perpetuation of threat in serial forms. Nothing changes. The irrational is not an escape from or subversion of the rational: it is only its obverse. An opposition which holds the pair in a dynamic equilibrium, the rational-irrational binary changes nothing. Singer's and Lee's Marvel films reprise the devout if wishful hope of *Princess Mononoke* for a reconciliation of opposing dynamics in the reconstruction of dialogue.

Of course, the mutations of X-men are mutations which result in speaking, communicating beings. Even so, Habermas' fear that eugenically manipulated offspring might sacrifice their equality in the dialogues of human community is here reversed into a fear – which the films seek to soothe – that the natural-born will be excluded, derided, deprived of their stake in the future. The avuncular Xavier may smack of the paternalism Habermas fears among parents of modified infants, a pitying, objectifying gaze grounded in the fact that the embryonic stage

X-Men: The X-men in their own environment – assured in their own alienation. Courtesy BFI Stills.

has indeed been objectified. There is no barrier to affection here, but it is the affection one might have for a domestic animal, a relationship in which one partner always retains the right to primacy over the other. Raised to the global scale of a war between species respectively more and less than human (most of *X-men*'s human characters are venal, self-seeking, timorous and weak).

Another variation in the *X-men* films: the mutations appear to have begun spontaneously. There may perhaps be a suggestion of environmental factors (the ubiquitous fear of atomic radiation in the earlier period of the comic books). But the mutations also appear to be transmissible, at least in the mythos of the comics of the early 21st century, where, intriguingly, Night Crawler is the unacknowledged child of Mystique, the shape shifter. Nonetheless, the struggle between Xavier and Magneto demonstrates two key qualities of the ethical world of the films: firstly, that dialogue, at least among mutants, is still possible, and secondly that such dialogue can also be conducted as war. The communication is still technologically mediated: various transport technologies, mobile telephony, plastic prisons, the Cerebro device. Slightly stranger, however, is the relative absence of weapons with, in their place, superpowers which, however, are also frequently introduced through gesture, a trait that may perhaps link them back to the gestural drawing of animals, a theme also picked up in the various characters who have difficulty controlling their powers, from Cyclops to Hulk. The superhuman is not yet supernatural. The categories of the communicative universe – physis, polis and techne – hold good yet.

In as much as the films form a parable about genetic modification, they fail in just this aspect. What marks the collapse of the moral world in Habermas is a collapsing distinction between what is human, what is natural, and what is technological. Where technology had the role of mediating between natural and human, in one direction applying human will to nature, in the other allowing nature to speak to humans, now it would appear from the analysis above of the political dimensions of the biotech industries, that the technology has achieved a kind of systemic autonomy. Neither consumers nor governments, not even corporations themselves, in hock to the demands of finance capital on the one hand and market competition on the other, have the will or the power to stop the development of genetic technologies. The return of the repressed is not just the swaggering of instinctive nature into the social: it is the explosion of repressed technology into society and nature.

This is at least the apocalyptic scenario of Virilio's 'genetic bomb'. The invention of the railway was, he argues, also the invention of the train wreck, the automobile of the car smash, the computer of data crash, and genetic engineering of biological collapse. To the extent that all our media, transportation, information and ecological systems are now networked in real time, the accident stops being a purely local or personal event, and becomes instead potentially global: the General Accident. Virilio here puns on the philosophical term 'accidence', an actually existing phenomenon which lacks the necessity of an absolute essence. Essential matters have become inessential, simulacra and simulations, and at the same time they have exploded. 'Apocalypse is happening all the time, every day since Genesis. It never stops. *Man is the end of the world*' (Virilio 2002: 154) he says, or, distinguishing carefully that he is addressing the labs rather than the gas chambers, 'Auschwitz was not only a crime against humanity: it is the beginning of the accident of science' (Virilio 2002: 153). For Virilio, there is a certainty, a destiny, involved in human affairs. Fallen humanity sets out on broken paths, all of which lead by crooked routes to the integral logic of their conclusions. To the extent that the project of Western science has been one of control, it has produced its opposite, a chaotic disorder, a *politique du pire*, a politics of the very worst (Virilio 1998).

For Virilio, who has followed an unorthodox but nonetheless professional career as an architect and urbanist, nature is what is lost in the process of building a synthetic world. For others it is wilderness, in the sense of reserved tracts of pristine nature. Other natures surround us: the residual wolf in Benjamin's dog; urban foxes and feral cats; the natural instincts of humans; the tilled fields of a rural landscape, the natality of the new born child. One way or another, none of these can claim purity. If by nothing else, the planet is bound together in criss-crossing communications by pollution, and the wilderness and the newborn are alike, at the molecular level, repositories for industrial waste. Our human being is composed of social currents that waft or rage through us, of organic processes we share with all the other animals, of environmental factors which, though we may cause them, we have little control over; and of technologies from speech to satellites that wind into the inmost areas of our most intimate dreams. Not even technologies are purely technical. The hybrid DNA technologies, nanomachines and computers powered by genomes examined by Eugene Thacker (2004) are at one extreme; at the other lies the embedding of human skills in the factory toolbox. One of the familiar defenses of genetic modification is that nothing essential has changed: humans have manipulated the species around them for millennia, using slower methods of selective breeding. All that has changed is that science today has a better understanding, and technology faster tools for implementing the same changes we have always made. The *X-men* movies are indeed apologies for genetic modification, but they do not pretend that they imply no change at all. If they fail it is because, despite themselves, they encourage the response of dread.

Which is not out of place for a film. The reality of change is, despite the rhetoric and the panic, far slower and less dramatic. Hatters died of mercury poisoning long before the aetiology of their madness was known to anyone, least of all themselves. From white lead to pesticides, people have crammed their bodies with change-inducing chemicals for at least a hundred years. Most people in the industrial world will by now have eaten battery animals reared on growth hormones and antibiotics, and dined on genetically modified soya, corn and other crops. Therefore the process of biopolitics, if it is the case that it must supersede bioethics, cannot be simply a question of reasserting human control over technological processes, since now the thresholds between technologies, nature(s) and humanities is no longer clear, and each has achieved a certain plurality. Drawing on his existential Catholicism, Virilio proposes an individualist response between the ethical and the political: 'That's what our job is', he argues, 'to wrestle with the genetic bomb as human beings – not as gods. To wrestle with the information bomb so as to produce something other than cybernetics. To wrestle with the atom bomb so as to avoid blowing everything to kingdom come. So I don't believe the world is finished, either. I am not a nihilist. I am simply saying that we have to fight like Jacob. Each person must wrestle with the angel' (Virilio 2002: 170).

Without his faith, a secular enquiry must to find another more secular virtue, and a more materialist understanding of the new communicational and systemic relations between the polis, physis and techne on which to ground it. In an aside, on the evidence of our complex relations with them, Habermas includes also the stillborn and the dead among the human community. To recall again Benjamin's 'weak messianic power', it is essential that such an understanding and its concomitant politics should embrace whakapapa, the generations before and to come, our posterity and those to whom we are posterity, who placed such hopes in us, and to whom we owe a debt. If there is a meeting of techne, polis and physis in the contemporary landscape, then we must also acquire some sense of the mutual responsibilities of each phylum to the pasts and futures of all three.

Always Take The Weather

Green Media, Global Change

Julius Caesar
Roman Empire
Couldn't conquer the blue sky
Crowded House

Herding Cats

Previous chapters have looked at a number of ways in which the natural environment and the media speak to, with or about one another. They have inspected the relationships between bio-security and cosmopolitanism, relations with and to animals, the use of technology as a medium through which the natural and the human can reach some kind of dialogue, the relationships between nature as fate and nature as destiny, the unhappy relations between ecoterrorism and a green public sphere, and finally the fraught zone of bioethics. Throughout I have wanted to voice a particular concern with the way in which, once constructed as an effective if fluid boundary, the distinction between human and natural, which cannot simply be annulled, may nonetheless be superseded by a new relationship, one grounded specifically in mediation. That mediation, I have intimated, is undertaken by neither physis nor polis, but by a third phylum, which I will continue to refer to as techne. This chapter aims to draw some of these ideas and arguments together around the proposal of the previous chapter, that if a bioethics may not be viable in a global system in which no grounding values can be presumed, then the alternative must be a biopolitics. The question about what form such a biopolitics might or should take requires another prior question as to whether the present can legitimately undertake to design such a biopolitics without abolishing the autonomous development of the future. How, in short, are we to balance our debt to our posterity against the requirement that we do everything in our power to free them of our more baleful achievements?

Greimas (1970) asked whether the natural world could mean, a question which he believed he had answered in the negative, convinced of the singularity of human communication. At least he had the courage to ask the question. The otherness of the world supplies scientific discourse with that unknown against which it pitches its knowledge, at the same time supplying aesthetics with that sublime, ineffable beyond which guarantees speech's transcendence of the world. The hypostasis of nature, while ostensibly condemning signification to misrepresentation, in fact constructs nature as the Other, fundamentally unknowable to the extent that, as object, it cannot be subject and therefore cannot signify.

The world then cannot represent: to paraphrase Marx, it must be represented. The naturalness of the world as other produces its silence, objectality and in-significance. To the extent that marginalised sectors of the world are rendered natural, they too are excluded from the world of speech, aesthetics and scientific reason. The slave, the colonised and women, privileged with the task of securing mere reproduction, sexual and home-economic, have shared in this silence. The polis of action, discovery and art has marked itself off as the counter-natural world of signification and significance.

But the world does nothing but signify. To be a world is to effervesce with an excess of signification. That this should be so is the product of an apparent contradiction: the world communicates because it is not whole. An axiom at the heart of Western philosophy since Aristotle, the proposition that A=A stands apparently absolute in its monumentality. Other axioms are possible. The pre-Socratic Heraclitus already knew that you cannot step twice into the same river because the river is not self-identical over time. In the three thousand year old Buddhist tradition, the world is illusion, perched between being and not-being. The world is not what it is. Europe's tradition from Aristotle to Kant distinguishes itself by its conceptualisation of being as identity. In the bright and battering revaluation of all values in the first industrial revolution, Marx, Darwin and Freud abolished that presumption. The logical category of identity could no longer apply when ideology, instinct and the unconscious left large tracts of the self unavailable to the self. The premise of non-identity was implicit in the new communications technologies, especially the cinema's illusion of motion through a trick of perception or cognition that bypasses the conscious eye and mind. By the beginning of the 20th century, the foundations of a social theory of self-identity, the ground of the distinction between world and human, could no longer be guaranteed.

20th century philosophy from Heidegger to Derrida identifies this movement from identity to the non-identical as a process of loss and lack: the loss of presence, the lack in being. Yet the process need only appear as a loss from the point of view of an identity which, in any case, may now appear to have always been illusory. Taking the non-identical as the ground of material existence explains why human being always exceeds the boundaries of a socially constructed 'self' where the social is of necessity a communication acting on and with others. There is no self to lose, split or lack, and there never was. Contemporary media and social theory is quite at home with this dissolution of the subject. Yet nature has rarely been considered in the same light. Social theory and political critique alike place nature in a position over against society, defined by its exclusion, and as Jody Berland insisted in a 2004 lecture, 'Cat and Mouse', even Deleuze and Guattari, in their becoming-animal thesis, disdain becoming anything as familiar and to their eyes devalued as a domestic cat or dog. Only the wild and strange were, she argues, animal enough for them. Human subjectivity is non-identical – fluid, schizophrenic, porous. But nature is pristine, pure, the perfect stranger.

Something dramatically similar seems to be believed of society. For Habermas, as we have seen, the loss of a community of equal selves threatens the very possibility of ethical action. And in a postmodern era, which offers only a plain of differences with no grounds on which to judge them, that prophecy might seem to have come to being. If, as Arendt feared, the rise of mass society spelt the end of glorious, history-making action and the rise of mere behaviour, a statistical aggregate like the movement of consumers from one product to another, then the current state of civil society is even more a supermarket of insignificant differences proliferating purposelessly under the invisible hand of the market. (That such glory and such making of history persists in other cultures is clear from the cult of the glorious Islamic martyrs. Our Western revulsion at their refusal of democratic means of argument, the mass statistic of voting, is emblematic of Arendt's case). Whether the homogenous unity of mass society or the meaningless differentiation of postmodernity, society is reduced to a single subject set over against Nature, and doomed, it seems, to eradicate both nature and itself.

The two processes – massification and the othering of nature – go hand in hand. For Neil Evernden, the beginnings can be found in the early scientific distinctions of the renaissance in which 'the discernment of meaning or purpose in Nature is to be treated as a conceptual pollution of reality' (Evernden 1992: 51). Stripped of Aristotelean final causes, nature no longer had the means to communicate with humans about the presence of God or its own healing powers. Instead, nature was to be the domain of laws, of physics and of cause and effect, a realm of necessity marked off from human freedom. In Kant a parallel necessity would emerge, 'since reason is not sufficiently serviceable for guiding the will safely as regards its objects and the satisfaction of all our needs (which in part it even multiplies) – a purpose for which an implanted natural instinct would have led us much more surely' (Kant 1964: 64). The renaissance mathematisation of nature – undertaken a scant century or so before mathematics would itself declare independence and strike out for its own autonomy – at the same time removed the sensuous and meaningful from the human-nature connection and instigated a new mysticism, that number should rule equally in the mind and in the mindless world beyond. In the still patrician and largely agricultural European Enlightenment, the division of nature and humanity seems, following Arendt, to be matched by a continuing division between the private world – private in the sense of 'deprived' – of natural processes like eating, sleeping and sex; and a public world of genuinely human activity, to which now was added experiment and scientific discourse.

The withering away of the private in the modern era concerns then the emergence of specialists in reproduction – the labouring classes – into public life. But the democratisation of the public sphere, like the democratisation of leisure, created in general a cheapened version of the old patrician preserve. And at the same time, the industrialisation of the reproductive cycle, the satisfaction of basic needs like shelter, food and clothing, further reduced the specificity of the private-natural world. Not even Marx thought of organising the women and children who tended the new manufacture: they were to be returned to their 'natural' place in the home, where children, despite their best efforts, still remain. This gives us one narrative, close to Berger's story of the gradual loss of intimacy with animals. Against the instrumentalisation of natural processes in the new capitalism, the Romantics sang up the resistance of wilderness to 'improvement', reinforcing the sense that the forests and mountains were the other of the factories and tenements. That dichotomy, so central to the growth of radical politics, must in the 21st century be brought back into question. We need a better history of the relations between peoples and environments than we can get from the pages of Wordsworth.

Environmentalism and Empire

Joseph Priestley's 'Observations on different kinds of air' of 1772 had quite a different impact, specifically on the emerging network of civil servants across the European colonies. As President of the Royal Society, Sir John Pringle was at the heart of these networks, noting of Priestley's scientific findings that 'From these we are assured that . . . every individual plant is serviceable to mankind if not always distinguished by some private virtue, yet making a part of the whole which cleanses and purifies our atmosphere'. (The dissenting Priestley also saw natural processes as models for political reform. Again in Pringle's account, the goal of storms was 'to bury in the deep those putrid and pestilential effluvia which the vegetables upon the face of the earth have been insufficient to consume', cited in Grove 1997: 132). When, in the 1763 Peace of Paris, Tobago, St Lucia, Grenada and St Vincent were ceded to the British, the Lords Commissioners provided for each island to include forest reserves 'for the protection of the rains' - Tobago's is still in existence – while the French physiocrat governor of Mauritius did the same in 1769 (Grove 1997: 10-11). Richard H Grove's analysis – which emphasises both the relative somnolence of the imperial metropolises and the readiness of the more enlightened colonists to learn from indigenous practice – sees a world-wide network of colonial meteorologists, arboricultors and botanical gardens developing from the mid-18th century that reached critical momentum at the Royal Geographical Society meeting of March 1865, when James Wilson called for 'stringent enactments' to protect vegetation in the colonies, a cause in which he was supported by Francis Galton, the founder of eugenics. The argument is premised on anthropogenic ethics: the colonies depended on adequate groundwater; deforestation was responsible for the drying up of springs and the loss of groundwater. What is intriguing about this phase of environmental awareness is less how early it began (Columbus is reported to have had similar fears after witnessing the desiccation of Madeira), and more that the concern was already global, and that it occasioned an early variant of authoritarian interventionism. The environment, it seems, only ever reveals itself in crisis.

A major El Niño event in 1790-1791 produced serious famine in a number of British colonies, several of them Treaty of Paris colonies, several of them neighbours to French colonies like Haïti, all of them subject to the winds of revolution from France and of the early antislavery movement in Britain. Perhaps administrators recalled the inference that the crop failures of 1789 had led to the French revolution, or that other environmental disaster, the explosive growth of the rat population and consequent Black Death of the 1470s, and its direct result in the shortage of farm labour and the Peasant's Revolt of 1481. Grove concludes that 'the first steps towards recognising . . .global influences and fluctuations were enabled and founded upon the relatively sophisticated networking of East India Company scientists . . . the periphery provided both initiative and innovation in extending human knowledge' (Grove 1997: 146). Landscape-changing policies were adopted as early as 1669 by Colbert in France, and from 1691 in New England, after the collapse of forest management ordinances in England due to intense pressure for naval construction (Malone: 1966; see also Schama 1995) and the relatively weak position of scientists vis-à-vis the emergent capitalist interest, a privilege largely reversed in colonial settings. In the colonies themselves, shifting alliances and confrontations between colonial state land managers, hunting enthusiasts among the colonial class, indigenous religious beliefs involving ecological stewardship, local comprador and landlord bourgeoisies, campaigns variously to 'civilise' or to control the activities of indigenous forest dwellers, and the agricultural and resource-extraction interests of colonial mercantile capitalists seem to have shaped the actual implementation of environmental policies, especially in forestry management and soil conservation, even in the 18th century.

The participatory, public scientific culture engaged in by a significant proportion of civil servants and colonial Company employees from the mid-18th century to the 1930s seems therefore to have played a significant part in a complex dialectic of interests in the building of environmental theory and political intervention in ecological matters. It is not so simple a matter as to blame science, or even imperialism, for environmental degradation, though certainly massive population shifts and the introduction of European farming methods and livestock must have added to the horrors of famines like that which, in the El Niño season of 1877-9, was estimated to have carried off fifty million in India alone. Struggles between state managers and farmers indicate that these impacts were already understood in the 1870s, and already disputed. Even the more liberal gestures of imperialists – for example campaigns against female infanticide – may have led to unsustainable population growth among forest dwellers, the consequent loss of habitat, and increased colonial policing and circumscription of traditional lifestyles. Endocolonial attempts at environmental management had an even longer history, from the enclosures to the draining of the fens, when common rights, of dubious ecological value, were fought for by riot and in Parliament for decades at a time. Likewise political campaigns of civil disobedience formed a kind of alliance with timber capitalists in pre-Revolutionary New England in resisting colonial forest conservation.

Even such a swift glimpse of the tendentious history of environmental management and rebellion suggest that a simple dichotomy, along the lines of Val Plumwood's (2002) argument, that a masculinist, instrumental science has enforced environmental degradation on peasants and indigenous peoples, is inadequate to understanding the nature of the conundrum. It also suggests that the simpler versions of the global-local dichotomy likewise fail to observe the actual dynamics of the constantly shifting struggles and alliances among varied interests over both local and global processes. Thirdly, there is clearly a history to the complex interweaving of economies and ecologies, a history which produces not only environmental disaster but genuine if often ill-judged, unpopular and dangerous political practices geared towards saving ancient habitats or preserving ecological equilibria. For example the planting of teak in the Malay States during the 1840s, stands now coming to maturity, echo distantly the foresight of the cathedral builders, who planted oaks at the time of consecration to provide replacement beams hundreds of years into the future. Fourth, the evidence would seem to suggest that left to democratic processes, the interests of the environment would, in the case of the British and French colonial empires, have fared even worse than they did under authoritarian intervention from the state, however much it was resisted by both popular and entrepreneurial factions. These last two points combine to suggest that democracy may not be the right road to an ecologically sustainable future. The thought would appear to be borne out by looking at the existing global and international agencies working in the environmental field.

The strongest case here is the murky process of agreements of global climate change management. The UN Environmental Programme (UNEP) sponsored the foundation of the Intergovernmental Panel on Climate Change (IPCC) in 1988, which reported in 1990 and 1995, the latter report including the now famous statement 'the balance of evidence suggests that there is a discernible human influence on global climate' (IPCC 1996, Summary for Policymakers). The guarded language is that of scientists, certainly, but also of diplomats cautious of overcommitting their governments. That same year, the UNEP established the Global Environmental Outlook (GEO) programme, which last reported in 2003, with outlooks for the period to 2032. GEO 2003 includes a commitment to the Malmö Declaration, composed at a major meeting of of environment ministers: 'The role of civil society at all levels should be strengthened through freedom of access to environmental information to all' (GEO3: 19). Even this modest request is proving hard to sustain within individual countries, let alone between them. According to the Waxman Report, the current Bush administration replaced the respected climatologist Dr Robert Watson as chair of the IPCC, apparently on the instigation of Exxon Mobil. In June 2003 the US government's Environmental Protection Agency annual report on the Environment was published without references to global warming after White House officials queried all mentions, and required the insertion of materials from a report sponsored by the American Petroleum Institute claiming that no such effects were measurable. Subsequent EPA reports to Congress have either not been forthcoming or have been incomplete where, according to the Waxman Commission, the analyses might have been damaging to White House policy. The House of Representatives (2003) report prepared for Rep Henry Waxman is a damning statement of the abuses of science and the potentially long-term damage done to the government scientific agencies by a single administration. If this is so in the relatively open democracy of the USA, how are weaker governments, even more deeply in hock to external commercial and diplomatic pressures, to ensure the free flow of environmental information to their politicians, let alone meet the Malmö Declaration's other goals of ensuring 'broad participation in environmental decision-making, as well as access to justice on environmental issues'?

It is widely argued that the power of nation-states is waning in the current development of globalisation. Governments are constrained by treaties, legal and technological protocols and agreements, the need to attract inward investment, to provide the kinds of internal policies in taxation, education, security, and environmental regulation that will bring in companies and financiers from overseas, a case that is true even of OECD nations like Canada, Australia and Aotearoa New Zealand (Kelsey 1999). Nonetheless, even in global decision-making bodies like the World Trade Organisation and the International Monetary Fund, governments are significant and often major players, even when they are constrained to speak on behalf of corporate interests.

At the same time, fairly typically, GEO3 lists 45 INGOs (International Non-Governmental Agencies) as collaborators in the report. Many of these are scientific agencies, but most of them represent specific geographical, habitat, even species-specific groups whose interests have to be sorted, balanced and conformed to one another in the effort to produce the significant science that can act as the basis for decision making. It seems probable that the process of reporting also requires a degree of self-censorship and trading of goals in the interest of successfully negotiated document that a majority of the partners can sign off on. Likewise there is no point in delivering a report which would be either dismissed out of hand by major power brokers or one which did not give decision makers options as well as room for further negotiation. The UN General Assembly's 1988 resolution on the climate as the 'common concern of mankind' established the grounds for discussion. The term 'common', however, evokes Garrett Hardin's 1968 essay on the 'tragedy of the commons', which argued for private ownership of common land, on the basis that common ownership would always lead to self-interested over-exploitation of grazing or woodland. The critical political meetings that followed – UNECD (Rio) in 1992, the Framework Convention on Climate Change (FCCC) ratification by the requisite 50 countries in 1994, the Kyoto Protocols of 1997, and the Buenos Aires plan of action in 1998 – would all in various ways debate privatisation and its alternatives (among them the carbon tax, quotas, and the trade in emissions).

According to Bodansky (2001: 28), the earliest phase was dominated by scientists and devoted to establishing that there was a problem. Once the governments became actively involved, the actuality, the significance and the actions required to deal with climate change became fraught, with the EU and the CANZ countries loosely in favour of limitation or reduction in carbon emissions, and the USA, joined at the time by Japan and Russia, against. The reasons for US reluctance seem to include, among other things, economic fears, a desire to appear as a tough negotiator on the world stage for other upcoming negotiations, fear of domestic electoral backlash, and internal struggles between the Reagan administration and the US Environmental Protection Agency. Each nation's response was similarly structured around the specifics of the local economy, the availability of clean or dirty carbon fuels inside their territory, desire to receive some benefit in return for agreement (or in more recent rounds non-agreement), geography (small island states were strong supporters of reduction), regional politics (India was not only developing its industrial base as a major political priority but also facing an increasingly belligerent Pakistan). And so on. In terms of domestic politics, in the unusual constitution of the USA, the Presidential signature is not automatically ratified by both houses, and a President without a rock-solid majority may not wish to risk a losing vote. That risk is compounded by the often observed drift from party loyalties to the interests of local electorates among elected members. The shift of environmental policy from Congress to the Executive has had significant repercussions, already noted of the Bush administrations attempt to make science correspond to ideological and in some instances at least economic policy. Equally byzantine political forces work in the EU, where European institutions, cross-border alliances and member-state domestic interests interact. Meanwhile 10,000 NGO delegates attended Rio, and 4,000 Kyoto, from at least 165 NGOs. Raustiala (2001: 100) lists, among attendees at one conference, the AFL-CIO, the Methodist Church, interest groups for tourism, fire control, alternative transport, consumer and environmental groups and the Uranium Institute as well as business consortia, some with potentially misleading titles like the Dow Chemical-led International Climate Change Partnership. Each one of these groups has to represent the negotiated position of a membership which is often riven between the common good and the competitive interests of its members. Nor is it surprising that the complexity of both international and NGO/INGO interests matches the complexity of the issues which they have set themselves to address. Like the confluence of the economic storm with the south-bending jetstream to form a single eco-economic catastrophe, the prospect of global climate change has met with a 250-year-old network of competing interests, temporary alliances and new enmities in a process which may have immense impacts on how, if at all, globalisation can be made accountable, and to whom.

Hollywood Ecology

Since Daniel Bell (1962, 1973), sociologists have been keen to include in their accounts of social cohesion the webs of voluntary action that citizens involve themselves with. Pressure groups, churches, unions and minority political parties attract passionate engagements, forge dynamic alliances, raise substantial amounts of money and dispose of them in inventive media and communication campaigns, in which environmental groups like Greenpeace have set the pace for imaginative, headline-grabbing activities. Music cultures, internet, 'zines, video distribution and other alternative media have become integral to the circulation of both radical and conservative attitudes towards global warming. Creativity may be as boundlessly abundant as Huxley believed nature to be; but there are limits to growth in the limited amount of time audiences can spare for entertainment and news. Cinema and television industries respond to political media and activities as both competitors for the limited attention of audiences, and as research and development zones, both for creatives and for new themes to pursue in their product. So Hollywood's attention to the development of green themes in popular culture is entirely true to form, not least because the people working in the industry, while constrained by the necessity to turn a profit, are also themselves citizens, as often as not as committed to social and environmental causes as their audiences. And, without labouring the production process in Californian film and television industries, its international recruitment, its hankering for the latest thing, and the labyrinthine roads through which projects pass on their way through development to release, another complex of negotiation and compromise, films either enter into dialogue with their audiences or they fail. That a film project will absorb at least two years from first draft to release adds a temporal dimension to the difficulty of analysing success in communication. Nonetheless, in these distillations of popular attitudes, it is possible to descry something of the workings of both the international negotiators and the ecological interactions that produce global warming through the production process and the affordances of interpretation, fandom and cultural bricolage, in the relatively simple phenomenon of a feature film.

Roland Emmerich's global warming disaster flick *The Day After Tomorrow* is in some ways a worthy attempt to reach a mass audience with the bad news about global climate change. In a rather unfair comparison, I want to contrast Emmerich's film with an earlier fiction film dealing with an environmental disaster. The Oklahoma Dustbowl of the mid-1930s in many respects changed utterly the environmental policies of the USA. It has its cinematic memoir in John Ford's *The Grapes of Wrath*. Like *The Day After Tomorrow*, most recent films of climatological armageddon – Luc Besson's *The Last Battle* for example, or the eco-apocalypse implicit in *Blade Runner*'s perpetual rain – are future disasters. Ford's film was, by the time it was made, an historical drama. Greg Toland's deep focus cinematography, and the elaborate staging in depth of the migrant camps, anchored the film in a popular memory already fixed through Woody Guthrie's songs and the photography of Walker Evans and the FDA. Ford's story, like the Steinbeck novel which it adapts, is about people, the human cost of the event and the human profiteers who lived off it. Not expressly concerned with the causes of the drought and the dust storms, it deals with the appalling conditions suffered by those who survived them. The experience of the past is held up as a warning to the future: an ancestral memory in formation. The epic scale collides with the dramatisation of working class lives, their depiction based on documentary photography largely familiar to its target audiences from the pages of *Life*. Articulating the realism of the film with popular memory, the cinematography and production design work to produce a film that was both effective political satire and an enactment of a shared tragedy. *The Grapes of Wrath* uses historical sources, including the novel and the photographs, to construct a memory out of which future actions can be constructed. Admittedly, the memory of a real eco-apocalypse remembered in *The Grapes of Wrath* appears to have been repressed in recent years with the clear-felling of ancient forest resumed in the USA. The success with which both the legacies of popular radicalism and the communications of the past to the future have been blocked in that country should indicate the vital rôle that tradition, popular memory and historical awareness can have; a rôle currently occupied instead by depictions of fictive and therefore debatable imaginary futures.

The Day After Tomorrow: Iconic destruction of the Hollywood sign. Courtesy BFI Stills.

This is the tactic of *The Day After Tomorrow*, whose spectacular effects dominate a storyline which has an outsider scientist, whose warnings have been ignored, trying to rescue his family from the sudden arrival of an ice-age in the Northern hemisphere. The formulaic plot is more comic-book than *X-men*, and clearly is not a major attraction for viewers. The film has sold on its effects: notable among them the devastation of Los Angeles by tornadoes. Scientific extrapolation is depicted as a warning first, and then as prophecy, as a vision of the End. The lesson of the Dustbowl is that ecological collapse creeps up gradually, its effects cumulative and always implicated in the economic and ultimately political lives of those who suffer it. Emmerich's film opts instead for vast and immediate overwhelming, and in place of popular memory recalls shots from other movies: the half-buried Statue of Liberty of *Planet of the Apes*, the lion guarding a snow-covered New York public library in *Twelve Monkeys*. The banality of the day-by-day experience of drought, famine, flood, pestilence and endless wars of attrition that characterise the onward march of greenhouse gasses are set aside. Understandably, this is a dramatic choice. But it also reflects a shift of concern from listening to the past towards fearing the future.

This is not to say that Emmerich has never addressed American history, whose popular recounting has shifted over recent years. The old Western, as myth of origin of the nation-state in the USA, was characteristically interested in westward expansion, in the civilising of the wilderness, and the preservation of wilderness values into the newly civilised. More recent films have been set in the eastern states, and in earlier periods. Apart from a cycle of Civil War films, including *Glory*, *Gettysburg* and most successfully *Cold Mountain*, these films have been set in the time of the French and Indian Wars and the War of Independence, where Emmerich's *The Patriot* is set. Unlike Michael Mann's earlier *The Last of the Mohicans*, *The Patriot* is warmly supportive of the civilising process. But like Mann, Emmerich situates his action firmly in the landscape, more rural than wilderness in the case of *The Patriot*, but even there recognisably a landscape held in equilibrium with the wild. The new costume drama version of American history permits an insight into how the natural world is pitched in relation to the political choices of the people who inhabit it, in these imaginings of the formative moments of the United States.

At the close of *The Patriot*'s first ambush, after Benjamin Martin (Mel Gibson) has been driven, against his will, to fight the English, the backstory of his rampage at Fort Wilderness begins to take shape. Catching the last fleeing British soldier in the back with a tomahawk, he starts in to hack his body in uncontrollable bloodlust. As his horrified sons look on, he abandons the attack, standing bloodied in sharp focus against the blurred backdrop of spring softwoods, the red firing against the green. A reverse shot of the three boys, shocked, aghast. Reprise of the previous view, reframing as Martin recalls himself and walks up from the stream where he let himself go rabid; cross-fade to a magic hour shot of horses, wagon and corpse among trees, low sunlight scattering as backlight through the saplings, a horn motif emerging from the strings as the shot is doubled by another take of the same scene, momentary double vision, the second take without Gibson, as if, before the fade to black, he had dissolved into the woods, a force of nature, the Green Man of English mythology becoming the Red Man of America.

Later, in the swamps at the Old Spanish Mission the militia gather, wild men of the hills. They spit, they eat dog. Frogs and cicadas surround their dialogue. Cut to the lawns of a plantation where Cornwallis is hosting a party to the strains of a string orchestra. The swamp waters are opaque and rippled with the activity of the men. The lake before the mansion is mirror calm and moonlight plays on the cottonwoods. Brittle laughter of painted duchesses, instead of the playful chortling of children that has accompanied Martin's rebel household and the village where the rebels find support. Cut to Cornwallis' dressing room, where he fusses over his uniform. The effete but honourable aristocrat discusses with the virile but dishonourable scion of a crumbled aristocratic house. At our next return to the swamp, defeated and dejected, Martin recounts the atrocity of Fort Wilderness to his son. The swamp is revealed as a flooded graveyard, a stone cross at centre screen with dry ice drifting from screen right. It is dawn on the swamp set, when Morgan Freeman struggles in with a wounded militiaman, the light from lanterns and from silver candlesticks stolen from Cornwallis adding touches of colour to the overarching blue. Cut to the English fort, and the testing of a trapdoor under a gibbet with three nooses. The cuts have progressed in their juxtapositions – from natural vigour contrasted with civilised superficiality, to nature red in tooth and claw set in opposition to the mechanisation of terror.

Before the final battle we are treated to an idyll in the Georgia sea-islands. Martin's children play in the sand with the black kids whose parents, they announced to the dragoons, were not slaves but free men. In the final sequence Morgan Freeman, whose character has gained his freedom as a reward for twelve months of service, and the other militia build a new house and a new world, together. The autumn colours of this final scene reply to the spring colours with which the film opened, grounding the narrative of war for independence in the untouchable sanctity of the seasons' round. The diurnal cycle of sunlight and moonlight, the annual cycle of the seasons, ground political history in and as myth. In another common figure in myths of national origin, a Yankee captain in the British army sets fire to a church in the archetypal act of betrayal, a theme of such stories from the Western to King Arthur. The portrayal of the birth of the nation as a kind of Vietnam, with the patriots in the place of the Vietnamese, is only part of its work. The central argument of the film is its mythopoeia, its sanctification of the founding of the United States in the agricultural mythos of the seasons, a sure as the circle of woods that bounds every estate we see in wide shot, sign of the legitimacy of the planter among the wilderness. The equation of Martin with the Red Man, through his blood-soaked face and his tomahawk, places him rather than first peoples as the natural inhabitant. At the same time, like the cowboys of old, he is the privileged mediator between European civilisation and American wild(er)ness in the building, literalised in the final scene, of a New World of equals.

That New World is, technically, synthetic: a synthesis of European law and natural fecundity in an ideology of freedom and equality. But as Lotman suggests, 'The fact that the unification of two different languages is achieved by a metaphor is proof of the essential differences between them' (Lotman 1990: 126). The resolution of the dialectic is unsafe if, as here, it is founded on a metaphor. The distinction between farmed land and forest is a defining feature of the wide shot in *The Patriot*, distinguishing also the two modes of war, open field battles and guerrilla attacks. Though the means be wild, the goal is arable. To this extent, only what can be brought into the arable can join the world of freedom and equality: the rest is in thrall to instinct – the laws of nature – and to that extent, like the evil dragoon, outside the law and thus unequal.

In *The Day After Tomorrow*, these balances are disrupted, and the narrative once more seeks to find a ground on which the perpetuation of the state can be secured. In this instance, the Vice-President who

The Day After Tomorrow: Narrative imbalance or death of narrative in the moment of apocalypse? Courtesy BFI Stills.

resists scientific advice is the betrayer, though he will see the error of his ways and repent before the end. Given the story's premise, there can be no reprise of the cyclical natural rhythms of the earlier film; instead the film employs many image types, from degraded video to scientific imaging, to build a sense of the unique as well as overwhelming character of the disruption. Other disruptions occur: the East-West orientation of the US political economy is tipped to a North-South relation. Experts and authorities become victims rather than saviours. And a marriage between science and action is arranged in the figure of the protagonist, an heir of Indiana Jones's blend of scholarship and derring-do. The crisis has as its central benefit that it makes possible once again the heroic action, even though there is no possibility of making a difference to the destined ice age. But the dramatic rescue that ends the film suggests that the devastation may be worth it if it restores to humanity the ability to act.

This is surely the basis for the opposition between the Vice-President and the scientist. The former takes stock of all the constraints, argues for economic, political, security and even moral restraint on the course of action that Quaid's scientist demands. Quaid by contrast is authoritarian, like most epic heroes, and wants the world to change without delay. He is the one who will take personal responsibility for the deaths of millions when he demands that everyone north of a line on the map be abandoned – and of course the one who risks his own life to rescue at least some of them. The Vice-President's consultative approach is shown as needless delay and vacillation when determined action is needed. The distinction rides on two factors: the familiar personification of political tendencies in US cinema, and the question of who is capable of seizing the moment and taking responsibility, here as so often equated with command. The flaw in the argument is that whatever the Vice-President decided, he would be unable to make a difference. There is no single person, not even a class, that can be held accountable, in law or politics, for global climate change. The decentring of rule within nations and in global polity is so profound, and the law so shackled by its legacy of individual blame, that no legal or political action can make a change. The loose, undefined but nonetheless general and practical knowledge that this is the case is addressed in the film's trust in authority, gained or restored. But the narrative resolution is hardly the point of the film. Audiences flock to see the devastation.

The popular mediation of ecological anxiety is not an exact science. If it were, every film and every TV show would be a success. Lack of marketing can explain failure, but even expensive marketing campaigns – like that for Emmerich's notable flop *Godzilla* – cannot guarantee box office returns on the scale of *The Day After Tomorrow*. As writer, director and producer, Emmerich can take a great deal of the credit, but he is unable to work without negotiating not only with the rival instincts of every other input to the film's financing and creative production, but with those of audiences. What is articulated in the fabric of the film is not just a generalised panic but a specific working-through of themes of aspiration as well as disaster, of the incongruities of future imaginings – the freighter drifting among skyscrapers – as well as the dark forebodings. The future is always envisioned in the eyes of the survivors, not of the nameless, numberless dead. In this case at least, the past is figured only as possession, a Gutenberg Bible clutched by a bibliophile in the frozen library. Losing the past is as deadly as gaining an unwanted future.

An Ecology of Media

Conclusions

I don't know how humanity stands it
with a painted paradise at the end of it
without a painted paradise at the end of it
(Ezra Pound, Canto LXXVI: 463)

Mediating

Under the night sky, microscopically clear in the southern hemisphere, it is hard to imagine any other universe. In those vast reaches are millions of galaxies, billions of stars, phenomena of terrible scale and bewildering strangeness; scales, energies and contingencies whose immensity commands humility. In all this sky, there is only one place where we can say with any certainty that there is life. If indeed we are the only experiment the universe has ever made with biology, we have some kind of cosmic duty to nurture it. Even if there does turn out to be some other place where life exists, we should be in a fit state to meet it when we get the chance. That photograph of the earth from the first lunar mission, so iconic for a generation, still haunts us. The last photograph ever taken in space (everything since has been transmitted electronically) grounds the green movement in responsibility for this isolated flash of colour in a darkling cosmos.

At any historical conjuncture, the meaning of what it is to be human is constructed from the relationship between nature and technology. Likewise, the meaning of nature is constructed out of the relationship between human and technological, and of technology from the relation between human and natural. The system is unbalanced. The technological is always at the negative pole in common talk: there is no equivalent there for the words 'unnatural' or 'inhuman', and it is technology which, most of all, is described with those epithets. Technology might appear to be recent, an addition to the relationship between human and nature, but it is in fact the nature of their separation and their articulation. Any work, as Marx understood, must first separate off a part of the world as object so that work can be done on it, and in that relationship the first chipped stones at once haul nature and humanity apart and remake their relationship anew.

In any work of signification, the same is true: all mediations separate what they rejoin in new configurations. Semiotician Juri Lotman has argued that human communication forms a semiosphere, a global conversation, internally divided, however, into smaller spheres, like cultures, which are intensely self-identified at their centres, but at their peripheries are more and more liable to the influence of neighbouring spheres. Their communication he describes as dialogue, arguing that 'the elementary act of translating is dialogue. Dialogue presupposes asymmetry' (Lotman 1990: 143) Moving beyond both Habermas' faith in a necessary equality, and Luhmann's belief in mutually exclusive functionally differentiated systems, Lotman grounds this statement in a prior axiom:

> Translation is a primary mechanism of consciousness. To express something in another language is a way of understanding it. And since in the majority of cases the different languages of the semiosphere are semiotically asymmetrical, i.e. they do not have mutual semantic correspondences, then the whole semiosphere can be regarded as a generator of information (Lotman 1990: 127).

Lotman restricts his analysis to the semiosphere comprised of all human communication. But what richness of information arises from the translations between those other communicating spheres, the natural and the technological, and their yet greater differences from each and from all human language.

Inhuman physis and unnatural techne would seem to be incapable of speaking with the human polis. Yet Lotman also argues, instancing the communication of a mother with her infant child, that 'the semiotic situation precedes the instruments of semiosis' (Lotman 1990: 144). The mere absence of a common code does not pre-empt the desire for dialogue: on the contrary, it spurs on invention of means for mediating between distinct and asymmetric entities. In the first instance such technologies as mathematics, experimental method and engineering may appear as impositions of human will upon a passive world. Yet in that same moment we must also descry impositions of the world on the formation of mediation: in wheeling stars, accidents of geology or meteorology like landslides and lightning strikes, and the sheer fact of gravity. Nature communicates with us as surely as we with it, but to do so it must mediate. Nature cannot tell us the idea behind a volcano in any way other than through a volcano. In this case it is not so much nature, nor even the volcano that speaks, but the same physical processes that work in the human body and its sensorium. Communication links what is common to what is not in an act of translation that is always inaccurate, to the extent that commonality is always, if only in minute particulars, different in each place from which it is experienced. Misunderstanding is written into translation, between languages and between phyla. But misunderstandings are the fundamental differences that make the semiosphere a generator of meanings.

This I take to be the core of Bauman's republican model:

> the most promising kind of unity is one which is *achieved*, and achieved daily anew, by confrontation, debate, negotiation and compromise between values, preferences and chosen ways of life and self-identification of many and different, but always self-determining members of the *polis* . . . an emergent unity which is a joint achievement of the agents engaged in self-identification pursuits, a unity which is an outcome, not an *a priori* given condition, of shared life, a unity put together through negotiation and reconciliation, not the denial, stifling or smothering out of differences (Bauman 2000: 178)

Bauman's democracy is a living, breathing network of many dialogues grounded in differences, differences which signify, and from whose interaction new conditions emerge, which have to be renegotiated in an unending debate. Nothing in this model is permanent except change. But can this model, which sounds idyllic at the level of small communities, be extended to the global scale? And given the arguments advanced in this book, can the members of the polis be described as 'self-determining' beyond the networks that, among other things, define them as members of the polis? If not, who belongs to the polis? Can citizenship be extended to future generations? Do the ancestors have a place in decision making? What about other phyla, who also suffer or thrive according to the decisions made in the polis? Can their differences also enter the realm of ecological politics? And if so, will they enter as equal partners? Barry Holden is guarded: 'the predominant view now does seem to be that there is a linkage between green political theory and democracy. Or, to put the point another way, that there is a linkage between environmental protection and democracy, such that democracy enhances protection of the environment, or, at the very least, that environmental protection and democracy are not incompatible' (Holden: 24).

Latour, whose actor-network theory analysed the delegation of agency in scientific research to technologies that to that degree achieve a certain autonomous agency in the lab, extends the theory of democracy to another class of agency: that of physis.

> I am asking for just a tiny concession: that the question of democracy be extended to nonhumans. But is this not at bottom what the scientists have always most passionately wanted to defend: to have absolute assurance that facts are not constructed by mere human passions? They believed too quickly that they had reached this goal by the short cut of *matters of fact* kept at the outset apart from all public discussion. Can one not obtain – more painfully, more laboriously, to be sure – a quite superior guarantee if humans

> are no longer alone in elaborating their Republic, their common *thing*? (Latour 2004: 223)

The discourse of rights among humans is most familiarly couched in the demand for control over the immediate neighbouring context in which life is lived – a city block, a nation, a state. These environs surround, as the word suggests, a prior actuality (as a context surrounds a text). That 'text', that prior actuality, is not the abstract species but concrete neighbours, and in an age of mass migrations, even a selected few among those. To make a false etymology, the environment environs the mental, a mentality which is hypostasised as culture, a common set of beliefs and values, a way of life which, in Raymond Williams' expression, is whole. Latour's investigations suggest that no human way of life is whole, entire unto itself. That is too the burden of systems theory and ecological sciences. Leopold's land no more stops at my skin than my consciousness stops inside the bone box at the top of my neck or at my epidermis, where it touches the world and the world touches me back. The assessment of values as the best achievable for the greatest number is founded on a mistaken belief: that the individuals or communities jostling for the good are either separate from one another or from the world that permeates them. The population of my lifeworld includes my intestinal parasites, my mitochondria, birds, trees and dandelions. It includes the fossil heritage that is daily set fire to and burnt off into the atmosphere. The strange chains of connectivity that link me to coffee farmers in Costa Rica also link me to thermophyle bacteria in the depths of the Atlantic Ridge.

A radio report during June 2004: a trucker from British Columbia was the 1300th person to stand atop Mt Everest. 'Take only photos, leave only footprints', but by now we know that even footprints are not without their systemic reverberations.

To emphasise mediation is to redefine democracy. Our global decision-making processes are caught up in hierarchies, from local electorates, through national governments, to international bodies; and from local firms to global INGOs that lobby the World Trade Organisation. Breaking through those hierarchies is going to be a long process, if it happens at all. And the withering away of the state which globalisation seems to be achieving is not a solution as long as states retain their geographical claims on resources and their use, and on the service of their people. Bureaucracy does not have to be seen as the rationalist enemy, a position as much associated with free market entrepreneurs as with Weber. In many ways the bureaucrats of residual state power are the last bastion of protection against corporate interests. But at the same time, the infamous failure of bureaucracies to communicate, even among humans, limits their action to conservation, a conservatism that preserves what has been achieved but is hard pressed to open itself to what remains to be done. The anxious attempt of *The Day After Tomorrow* to ward off a future which is in any case predestined is in many respects the voice of bureaucratic conservationism. The challenge is to restore to futurity a sense of hope.

It may be that we need to let go: to allow evolution to take its course. To accept that not only humans migrate. That though we have certain obligations as citizens of the planet, so do other species, including perhaps the transgenic and the cyborg. Hybridising diasporas may be the best response to conservationist globalisation. In any case, if there is to be a future at all, then 'quality of life' will have to include all qualities and all lives. A planetary democracy will be mediated or it will not be. Those media will be increasingly not only technological but biological, as the ozone hole communicates from the Northern hemisphere to the Southern. Perhaps we can find a more interesting message to send than 'get cancer and die'.

Distribution

Ecological thinking places the emphasis on the priority of systems over nodes. In that case, power arises only from the system, whether that system be exclusively human polis or a polis that embraces the land. The question then arises: why do we give power to the powerful? This is a historical question, because it asks how the semiosphere evolved in such a way as to provide for the blockage of flows (accumulation, deferral, denial, derailing . . .). Why do people give power to Exxon Mobil? We cannot blame Exxon for exercising what we seem so freely to donate. On the same grounds of the system being the source of all energies, and further to the ecological conceptualisation of the system as fundamentally communicative, another historical question: how did we arrive at a system which thrives on the market in attention (Smythe 1994)? In the ecological perspective embraced here, it is axiomatic that everything, humans of course but the whole world, generates meanings. That being the case, we cannot blame the media for the attention we give them. Media citizenship means taking responsibility for generating meanings. This may require more than the bricolage of aberrant decoding. An ecology of media adequate to the complexity of the ecosystem requires citizens communicating. (Mother was right, about media if not about bullies – ignore them and they will go away). The political issue is not how to get wealth and power from the rich and powerful, as if wealth and power were objects they could own. Money and influence are systemic qualities – money is communication, power is communication, not things that can be owned. What generates wealth? The ecosystem and the work that ordinary people do on it. We have to learn to stop giving our money away to nodes of the network where it is amassed, and because it stops circulating, stops communicating. It is not a question of taking money from the wealthy: it is about stopping giving it to them day after day after day. Ditto power, and ditto mediation.

There is a powerful argument against Green policies that ecopolitics is a luxury for those who can think ahead to the future. For the poor and brutalised, survival takes precedence. Below-subsistence poverty is the single largest enemy of ecological movements, and cannot be ended by the eugenic ecoauthoritarianism of population control by famine, as advocated by some of the more brutal 'survivalist' greens. Castells (1996: 133-6) talks about the vast tracts of sub-Saharan Africa as supernumerary to the requirements of globalisation, nations whose raw materials are of diminishing significance, whose populations have no education and therefore no creative value in the emergent information economy, and which can therefore be left to starve or die of AIDS. A philosopher could call it 'the real world', and the Real, as Lacan says, is impossible. The Symbolic does not hold sway: not political dialogue, not the circulation of money, scarcely the circulation of food, and because of that scarcity precious little of the wealth of the ecosystem. We might complain that our world is over-symbolic, but to inhabit a region where symbolic action is impossible, excluded from the global communication of food, clothing, hospitality and trade is far worse. For genuine global democracy, for equitable distribution of wealth and access to decision-making, and for the survival of the planet to be possible, that brutal reality has to end.

Which would appear to be a double-bind. Poverty requires wealth, and since the wealthy – the middle classes of the developed world – are not likely to give up either their riches or their addiction to carbon fuels, increasing wealth implies more pollution. Moreover access to wealth requires education, which devastated countries cannot afford and immiserated populations cannot prioritise. Improving the situation demands the creation of a political class who can carry their arguments to the world stage, but such classes by the nature of things become increasingly remote from the populations they represent. What an ecologically informed concept of mediation has to offer is not a solution but an understanding: that these spheres of activity – economics, politics, education and the rest – are mutually informed and informing; that together they constitute a semiosphere, and that that semiosphere is by no means remote from the fortresses of Europe and North America. Emphasising the connections is not so much an ethical appeal as a mere fact. Where there is poverty, the simplest thing to do is move to where there is wealth. Where the environment is collapsing, the simplest thing to do is go where the green plants are. Currently the systemic response is to try to close down population movements, to block the flows. By and large the result is that those forced to stay behind sink into war over control of the dripfeed of aid and its openness to corruption: an ethics of survival that, to the cynical, appears to justify the effective imprisonment of the poor, whose survivalism proves that they are unworthy. Mediation theory suggests only that blockage and accumulation are systemically dangerous, and that a damaged system does not only harm the region where crisis begins.

The cases examined in the present work began with the expression of anxiety over bioregionalism and fear of flows; arguing that technology has begun to emerge as a means for mediating between polis and physis. In such fields as economics and politics, ecology is not only the content of debates but the form of economies and policy-making, inextricably interwoven with them. In the later part of the book, arguments are raised towards reintroducing the past into what otherwise too often appears as a spatial issue, the structure of systems rather than their traverse through time. That attention to the past is especially necessary when the environment appears as crisis, a crisis that in various ways denies the possibility of a future. Deprived of the grounds for a moral judgement, a secular concept of mediation must understand its ethics as politics, as an activity that embraces multitudes of constraints and voices, that is driven by difference. Crucial among these differences are those that distinguish polis, physis and techne. The art of the possible, politics cannot be driven by ethics, since the grounds of ethics cannot be shared across phyla, and are no longer secure even within the polis. The destiny and panic presented by Green and anti-Green are not alternatives to a failed moral universal: they are its irrational obverse. Neither apocalypse nor utopia will arrive the day after tomorrow. The process is longer, slower, more banal. The heroic gesture has not only been overwhelmed by sheer weight of numbers, but has been reduced to acts of terror and tyranny. Increasing the scale of Bauman's dialogic democracy means also slowing down. The burthen of mediation as a perspective on the global politics that will be required if the three phyla are to survive is that all of our communicating is germane, even the most apparently trivial. Welling up from popular media are visions and stories that unveil a common awareness of complexity. Sloganeering is no response. The yearning and the love are real enough, as are the fears, and most of all the sense that the world has grown into a fabulously interconnected web. Understanding the political as communication suggests tasks of opening up the closed meetings, unlocking closed information, sharing knowledge and ensuring that peripheries and borders are recognised as critical sources of the new.

The discourse of rights that is thrown into crisis in contemporary global capitalism is essentially legal: a discourse whose closest parallels lie in the rights of consumers. Distinct from them are the responsibilities of citizens, yet these responsibilities, which take the form of ethical obligations, are themselves thrown into crisis by the lack of a universal right beyond the economic. In the globalisation process hurried equally by the geographical expansion of capitalism and the intertwining of ecologies, a third figure arises, the migrant, shorn of rights, with limited access to citizenship. The migrant however has the unique freedom which Flusser ascribes to her: freedom from habitual rights and duties, and freedom to construct them anew, either on return home or in committing to a new place. In systems terms, the migrant's border crossings are the place of translation and information. Not that migration is new, far from it. Perhaps only slaves and convicts have been as imprisoned on a tiny patch of ground as the European feudal peasantry, and perhaps that is why, once freed of feudal bonds but unaccustomed to the open dialogues of traders and pilgrims, they became the colonists and settlers of later epochs. The principle of non-identity holds good of human populations too, save when the needs of wealth and power required an ideology of identity. The new migrants, burdened with all their histories, now face the often bitter task, not only of leaving, but of arriving to build a different world.

Migration is a medium. Like the great migrations of animals, human migration moves not only biomass but everything that travels with animals: their pests, their dung, their diseases and their genes. But animals, including humans, are not only media: they are senders and receivers, nodes in an increasingly interwoven webwork of communication, whose mediations they perform in their bodies and their technologies. Translated from here to there, they are also translators. Metaphorically at least, in our lack of self-identity, and uprooted from the old universals, we are all migrants now. This broken subjectivity is a consequence of the repression of history, but it is also by the same token an opportunity for the migrant's freedom. *Screen* theory of the 1970s proposed the socialisation of subjectivity, its diffusion into structures and networks of human interaction, but the theory of representation it rested on was unable to ask the subsequent question: the status and nature of objectivity.

The theme of subject and object that bedevilled modernity from Descartes to Lacan structures both the individual-society dialectic of sociology and political science and the relationships between individuals and their technologies. It is by now a truism that societies shape individuals and that technologies both express and inform relations between individuals. We know too that 'language speaks us', and that techne – technologies and languages alike – are the ossified layering of the ages of previous human relations and activities. Ecological thinking asks us to confront in addition the relationships of society at large and of individual subjects with the non-human world of nature. This requires consideration both of what kind of object nature is, and therefore what kind of subjects we are for nature, and what relationships produce these specific subject-object constellations. To engage in green politics involves both articulating policies designed to protect and enhance the natural world, and altering social and individual relationships with it. At both social and individual levels, this implies taking responsibility for what becomes of our relationship with nature. At the policy level, this seems relatively straightforward. Laws restricting toxic dumping can be formulated, enacted and enforced. But at the level of the individual, there is a crux in the current state of ideas about subjectivity that makes the issue of responsibility treacherous. If indeed the world is constructed by subjects who are themselves constructions of their social, technical and natural environments, in what sense can subjects take responsibility – for themselves or for the green environment?

Mediation can be analysed in three moments: the production of objects, the audiencing of subjects, and distribution that carries information between them. Production is the work of shaping the physical attributes of matter and energy in space and time; and vice versa, giving physical actuality to dimensions. Audiencing is the work of attention that gives energy and matter significance. Physical stuff requires this work of audiencing to recognise it as an object, but more fundamentally to produce its informational value by assessing its probability in relation to all other objects, its signal-to-noise ratio. Distribution mediates between these activities. On the one hand it conveys objects to subjects, as for example a television broadcast does. On the other, it conveys data about subjects back to the production process in the form of ratings, market research, awards and critical reviews. At the same time as it opens channels and maintains the address of objects to audiences, distribution must in that act also differentiate them. Distribution is then the moment of communication charged with establishing the both the difference and the communication between subjectivity and objectivity. Itself a construct of the process of analysis, distribution emphasises the flow of communication from there to here and back again.

History, considered now as the history of human communication, is generated at two moments of the mediation cycle, the moments of audiencing and of distribution, which meet where the one generates and the other manages significance, the informational content and value of communicated objects. In any form of trade and exchange, distribution is the zone which, in governing flows, has the power to block them and to amass their content. Citing the legal philosopher Drucilla Cornell to the effect that 'what is most characteristic of our humanity is that we are dialogical or conversational beings in whom language is a reality' (Cornell 1985), Rosemary J Coombe argues that 'we [legal anthropologists] need to examine the differentiated power that social agents have to make their meanings mean something, and the material factors that constrain signification and its circulation in contemporary societies' (Coombe 1998: 47). The role of distribution then is not only to transmit but to block, control, regulate and amass flows in time and space. From the Eleusinian mysteries to secrets of state, power, wealth, patriarchy, all our distinctions, exploitations and oppressions arise from control over the distribution of communication flows. In contemporary media industries that means control over what gets to market and when; who gets paid and when; who can access the vast databanks of information about audiences characterised as consumers and when, and so who can get into the market in the first place. From physical transport to micromarketing, distribution is the key to power, control, and the amassing of wealth. In distribution the selection, targeting and construction of audiences is reciprocated in the overdetermination of the production of objects for them. This is how the regulatory function shapes the media formations in which we live and between which we move. Even at the interpersonal level, secrets, betrayals and lies are the tools of mastery; and the ability to lie to oneself is not just a survival mechanism but an integral part of the pact every consumer makes in every purchase, and too often how we justify injustice in ourselves.

Responsibilities

It would be simplistic to see nature as productive, humanity as subject and technology as the distributive agency dividing and ruling them. The temptation to do so arises precisely from the domination of the commodity form, and the position of money and specifically of profit as the dominant mode of communication in the contemporary world. But precisely for this reason it is vital not to attribute universality to capital or to the human/non-human relation as that of subject and object. If the constructivist argument holds good, then arguing the universality of the commodity makes it universal, and reduces struggle against it and for alternatives to mere resistance against an irresistible force.

Granted that nature is a construct, nonetheless it is constructed out of the same raw materials as human communication – physical, dimensional and informational. And if it has been constructed, and comes down to us as the multiple overlayering of all the relations we have entered into with the non-human world, nonetheless it can be reconstructed. What Marx said of history can be said equally of the environment: people make nature, but not under conditions of their own choosing. Nonetheless, as the founding of the Communist Party demonstrated, people do make history, and they can remake nature. But the obverse can also be true. If humans were the producers of objects and the natural environment their interpreter and consumer, what then? Lovelock's (1979) Gaia hypothesis is a familiar example of this green logic: constrained to consume what humanity produces, nature as subject creates a history and a future in which humans may have no part. Nature in this instance takes responsibility for itself, but not for us. Its intelligence and agency are inhuman.

The problem of inhuman subjectivity and agency reflects back on the initial question: what constitutes a human subject capable of taking responsibility? The Gulf War and the invasion of Iraq were both widely criticised as instruments of the oil cartel so richly represented in George W Bush's cabinet. Though the official version presented Hussein as the villain, for many the parties precipitating conflict were the oil companies seeking access to the Caspian, and demonstrators around the world were unafraid to say so. What was and is far harder to find is anyone willing to give up their addiction to the internal combustion engine. Boycotts of BP or Shell are not damaging to the industry as a whole as long as people still buy petroleum from someone. Human individuals rarely take responsibility for their own wastage of an irreplaceable petrochemical fossil heritage. They are, in what I take to be a technical term, sentimentalists, who would enjoy the anger against Exxon and pity for the seabirds destroyed by the Valdes, without taking responsibility for what happened. To blame corporations is to deny agency to subjects; to claim the necessity of driving automobiles is to accept the dominance of the industry that more than any other is responsible for ecological catastrophe, warfare and global warming. The only alibi is the predestinarian one: the schizophrenic subject has no way of accepting personal responsibility, since it is a construct of other and older formations over which it has no power.

Agency then does not lie in human individuals, nor in vast, glacially slow-moving media formations like capitalism, in corporations, cartels, the oil industry or the WTO, nor in a nature invested with the responsibility for the environment that a denatured humanity no longer feels it can achieve. Agency lies in the field of distribution, the communicative structures operating in the subject-object relation. Buffeted by all the claims of all the media formations that focus on constructing and perpetually reconstructing them, individuals are too fragmentary, weak and overburdened to be able to undertake the tasks of changing the world. But if it is the case that individuality is a function of a specific constellation of the communicative cycle, then it is open, if not to change in itself, at least to communication with others. Such kinds of communication are perpetually being invented, expropriated, closed down, commercialised and abandoned, from pirate radio and xerox art to BBS and cellphone trees. The emergence of the Greens as a major political movement in the period since Lyotard (1984) wrote about the end of the *grands récits* is a story of communication, a type for Hardt and Negri's (2000) concept of multitudes (in a book deeply flawed by its ignorance of contemporary mediation).

The dominant mode of thought in the early 21st century is scientific, a diverse and internally conflicted raft of discourses which however share certain premises, among them the capacity of the human mind to know something of the true existence of the rest of the universe. Not all scientists deny the possibility that the universe in turn knows about us – Heisenberg's uncertainty principle implies that the presence of observers alters physical processes. It is not my intention to deny that knowledge is possible; only to suggest that it is a secondary effect in the communication between humans and their environments. Fundamentally mathematical in orientation, science nonetheless invents the math it needs to describe what it finds, and mathematicians are unabashed at inventing counterintuitive, even apparently counterfactual constructs.

Such generating of possibilities which nature may or may not come to fit with is a good example of the mutuality of human and natural productivity, their feedbacks, mutual determinations and inspirations, their misunderstandings, in short their communication. The inference is that physis, the stuff the world is made of, is already a communicating universe, composed as much of information, and therefore of differences that signify, as is the human or the technological.

A media formation is permeable to other formations as an individual subject is permeable to other subjects, and by extension a media object is permeable to other media objects, their intertwining the characteristic effervescence of the communicative. Hatred, fear, anxiety, avarice, vainglory, lust, vengeance, the deadly sins are deadly because they arrest that generosity, turn it to mastery, hoarding, waste. Even were it a possibility, there would be no point to the atavistic desire to return to older and simpler ways, to reunite with the green world or to abandon the social for the instinctive. Poor, nasty, brutish and short, those lives in which subjectivity was as yet ill-formed, and objects indistinguishable from each other and from any sense of self. That infantile, pre-rational world of emotions vast as heaven is well left behind. The task of thinking mediation is not to idolise a remote past but to build, brick by brick, a new future. Abrams (1971) argued that history was for the Romantics a spiral climb back to the beginning. For our generation it is the hard haul, if we survive so long, to a different beginning.

In his remarkable study of the roots of human culture, Jared Diamond (1997) insists on the primacy of fits between environment and development. Only in those parts of the world where flora and fauna had the right qualities to become domesticated could fixed agrarian communities, chiefdoms and states develop. Only those crops and creatures that could be transplanted across the East-West axes of similar habitats encouraged the growth of trade and empire. And where, as in the Fertile Crescent, the early civilisations overtaxed the land with irrigation and intensive grazing, the great leaps forward petered out in saline soils and desertification. What leaps out from Diamond's study is the necessity of listening and learning from the green world. Domesticable beasts are herd animals who will imprint on a human the rôle of pack leader, who will, in other, words, communicate with humans. Others communicate by attacking, scavenging or becoming parasitic.

In our own way, even modern Western cultures listen to the world, though the professionalisation of science exaggerates the gap between common sense and expertise in ways that are less clear in traditional societies. Since the Chaldean astrologers and the builders of Stonehenge, the skies have talked to us. There is no question, then, of restoring a lost dialogue with nature. That dialogue has never ceased.

To the extent that we are also embodied creatures, nature's tides flow in our biorhythms, her food in our flesh, her drugs in our brains. The absolute distinction between nature as environment and the second nature of technology and technique is hard to locate. And yet we sense that division, seek remedies for it in New Age philosophies and tourism, and explanations for it in our media. The question is not 'how do nature's communications flow through us?' but 'what stops them?'. Somewhere in the distribution of communication, a wavering, permeable but tangible line separates humanity from world. Much of this book concerns the ways in which contemporary media have thought through this division, assembled fantastic myths of union, summoned visions of harmony, composed bleak elegies for the end of fellowship between the green and technological worlds. Beneath these themes lies another and more utopian one: that human communication is only comprehensible in relation to the universe of communication that enfolds, contains and speaks with it. The mutuality of the moments of communication leads to another possibility: that nature might stand in the place of distribution, articulating *homo faber* with *homo sapiens*. Could it be that nature is none other than mediation, and that the permutations in our conceptions of both are the histories of an integral communication to which we may yet aspire?

Bibliography

Abrams, M.H. (1971), *Natural Supernaturalism: Tradition and Revolution in Romantic Literature*, Norton, New York.

Agamben, Giorgio (1998), *Homo Sacer: Sovereign Power and Bare Life*, trans Daniel Heller-Roazen, Stanford University Press, Stanford.

Agamben, Giorgio (2002), *The Open: Man and Animal*, trans Kevin Attell, Stanford University Press, Stanford.

Althusser, Louis (1965), *Pour Marx*, François Maspéro, Paris.

Altman, Rick (1999), *Film/Genre*, BFI, London.

Appadurai, Arjun (1996), *Modernity at Large: Cultural Dimensions of Globalization*, University of Minnesota Press, Minneapolis.

Appadurai, Arjun (2002), 'Deep Democracy: Urban Governmentality and the Horizon of Politics' in *Public Culture* v. 14 n.1, 21-47.

Arendt, Hannah (1958), *The Human Condition*, University of Chicago Press, Chicago.

Bakhtin, Mikhail (1981), *The Dialogic Imagination: Four Essays*, trans Caryl Emerson and Michael Holquist, University of Texas Press, Austin.

Balibar, Etienne (1991), 'Is There a "Neo-Racism"' in Etienne Balibar and Immanuel Wallerstein, *Race, Nation, Class: Ambiguous Identities,* (trans of Etienne Balibar by Chris Turner), Verso, London, 17-28.

Barnett, Steven and David Doherty (1986), 'The Peacock Debate in the UK' in *Screen*, v.27, n 3-4, May-August, 24-28.

Barry, John (1999), *Rethinking Green Politics*, Sage, London.

Barthes, Roland (1980), *La chambre claire*, Gallimard, Paris.

Bateson, Gregory (1973), *Steps to an Ecology of Mind: Collected Essays in Anthropology, Psychiatry, Evolution and Epistemology*, Paladin, London.

Bauman, Zygmunt (2000), *Liquid Modernity*, Polity, Cambridge.

Bazin, André (1971), *What is Cinema?*, Volume 2, trans Hugh Gray, University of California Press, Berkeley.

Beck, Ulrich (1995), *Ecological Politics in an Age of Risk*, trans Amos Weisz, Polity, Cambridge.

Bell, Daniel (1962), *The End of Ideology*, Penguin, Harmondsworth.

Bell, Daniel (1973), *The Coming of Post-Industrial Society: A Venture in Social Forecasting*, Basic, New York.

Benjamin, Walter (1969a), 'Theses on the Philosophy of History' in *Illuminations*, ed Hannah Arendt, trans. Harry Zohn, Schocken, New York, 253-264.

Benjamin, Walter (1969b), 'The Work of Art in the Age of Mechanical Reproduction' in *Illuminations*, ed Hannah Arendt, trans. Harry Zohn, Schocken, New York, 217-251.

Benjamin, Walter (1979), 'Theologico-Political Fragment' in *One-Way Street and Other Writings*, trans Edmund Jephcott and Kingsley Shorter, New Left Books, London, 155-6.

Benjamin, Walter (1979a), 'Critique of Violence' in *One-Way Street and Other Writings*, trans Edmund Jephcott and Kingsley Shorter, New Left Books, London, 132-154.

Bleakley, Alan (2000), *The Animalizing Imagination : Totemism, Textuality, and Ecocriticism*, St. Martin's Press, New York.

Blühdorn, Ingolfur (2000), *Post-Ecologist Politics: Social Theory and the Abdication of the Ecologist Paradigm*, Routledge, London.

Bodansky, Daniel (2001), ' The History of the Global Climate Change Regime' in Urs Luterbacher and Detlef F. Sprinz (eds), *International Relations and Global Climate Change*, MIT Press, Cambridge MA.

Bookchin, Murray (1996), *The Philosophy of Social Ecology*, rev ed, Black Rose Books, Montreal.

Brereton, Pat (2004, forthcoming), *Hollywood Utopia: Ecology in Contemporary Hollywood Cinema*, Intellect, London.

Broberg, Gunnar and Bent Sigurd Hansen (eds) (1996), *Eugenics and the Welfare State: Sterilization Policy in Denmark, Sweden, Norway and Finland*, Michigan State University Press, East Lansing.

Caillois, Roger (1984), 'Mimicry and Legendary Psychasthenia', trans John Shepley, in *October* n.31, Winter, 17-32.

Callicott, J Baird (2001), 'The Conceptual Foundations of the Land Ethic' in Louis P Pojman (ed), *Environmental Ethics: Readings in Theory and Application*, Wadsworth, Belmont CA., 126-136

Castells, Manuel (1996), *The Information Age: Economy, Society and*

Culture volume One, *The Rise of the Network Society* , Blackwell, Oxford.

Caughie, John (2000), *Television Drama: Realism, Modernism and British Culture*, Oxford University Press, Oxford.

Clark, Nigel (2002), 'The Demon-Seed: Bioinvasion as the Unsettling of Environmental Cosmopolitanism' in *Theory Culture and Society* v.19 n 1-2, 101-25.

Coe, Brian (1981), *The History of Movie Photography*, Ash and Grant, London.

Commoner, Barry (1971), *The Closing Circle: Nature, Man and Technology*, Alfred A Knopf, New York

Conley, Verena Andermatt (1997), *Ecopolitics: The Environment in Poststructuralist Thought*, Routledge, New York.

Coombe, Rosemary (1998), *The Cultural Life of Intellectual Properties: Authorship, Appropriation and the Law*, Duke University Press, Durham NC.

Corea, Gena (1986), *The Mother Machine: Reproductive Technologies from Artificial Insemination to Artificial Wombs,* Harper and Row, New York.

Cornell, Drucilla (1985), 'Towards a Modern/Postmodern Reconstruction of Ethics' in *University of Pennsylvania Law Review* 133, 291-380.

Council of Europe (1997), *Convention on Human Rights and Biomedicine*, http://conventions.coe.int/treaty/en/treaties/html/164.htm, accessed 12 May 2004.

Crary, Jonathan (1999), *Suspensions of Perception: Attention, Spectacle and Modern Culture*, MIT Press, Cambridge MA.

Cubitt, Sean (1997), 'David Attenborough' in Horace Newcomb (ed) (1997), *Encyclopedia of Television*, vol 1, Fitzroy Dearborn, Chicago, 101-103.

Cubitt, Sean (2001), 'The Art of Partition: Globalisation, Diaspora and Ecological Aesthetics' in Bryan Biggs, Angela Dimitrakaki and Juginder Lamba (eds), *Independent Practices*, Bluecoat, Liverpool, 60-71.

Cubitt, Sean (2002), '*Delicatessen* or Eco-Apocalypse' in Sean Cubitt and Ziauddin Sardar (eds), *Aliens R Us: Postcolonialism and Science Fiction*, Pluto Press, London, 2002, 18-33.

Deleuze, Gilles and Félix Guattari (1980), *Mille plateaux* (*Capitalisme et Schizophrénie II*), Editions de Minuit, Paris.

Diamond, Jared (1997), *Guns, Germs and Steel: The Fates of Human Societies*, Norton, New York.

Dienst, Richard (1995), *Still Life in Real Time: Theory After Television,* Duke University Press, Durham NC.

Duster, Tory (2003), *Backdoor to Eugenics*, 2nd edn, Routledge, New York.

Eco, Umberto (1986), *Faith in Fakes: Travels in Hyperreality*, trans William Weaver, Minerva, London

Elmer, Greg (2004), *Profiling Machines: Mapping the Personal Information Economy*, MIT Press, Cambridge MA.

Enzensberger, Hans Magnus (1988), 'Critique of Political Ecology' in *Dreamers of the Absolute: Essays on Ecology, Media and Power*, Radius, London, 253-295.

Evernden, Neil (1992), *The Social Creation of Nature*, Johns Hopkins University Press, Baltimore.

FAO (Food and Agricultral Organisation Information Group) (2002), *The State of World Fisheries and Aquaculture 2002*, FAO, Rome.

Feuer, Jane (1983), 'The Concept of Live Television: Ontology as Ideology' in E Ann Kaplan (ed), *Regarding Television*, American Film Instute Monographs 2, University Publications of America, Frederick, MD., 12-22.

Flaubert, Gustave (1976 [1881]), *Bouvard and Pécuchet*, trans AJ Krailsheimer, Penguin, Harmondsworth.

Flavelle, Dana (2004), 'Monsanto Drops Modified Wheat', *Toronto Star*, May 11, D1, D13.

Flusser, Vilém (2002), *Writings*, ed Andreas Strohl, trans Erik Eisel, University of Minnesota Press, Minneapolis.

Flusser, Vilém (2003), *The Freedom of the Migrant: Objections to Nationalism*, trans Kenneth Kronenberg, ed and intro Anke K Finger, University of Illinois Press, Urbana.

Foucault, Michel (1976), *Histoire de la sexualité, 1: La volonté de savoir*, Gallimard/NRF, Paris.

Freud, Sigmund (1977), 'Fetichism' in *On Sexuality - Three Essays on the Theory of Sexuality and Other Works*, trans James Strachey, ed Angela Richards, (= Pelican Freud Library 7), Pelican, Harmondsworth, 345-357.

Fukuyama, Francis (1992), *The End of History and The Last Man*, Free Press, New York.

Gandy, Oscar H Jnr (1993), *The Panoptic SortThe Political Economy of Personal Information*, Westview Press, Boulder CO.

George, Susan (1992), *The Debt Boomerang: How Third World Debt Harms Us All*, Pluto, London.

Giedion, Siegfried (1948), *Mechanisation Takes Command: A Contribution to Anonymous History*, Norton, New York.

Gott, Richard (1989), 'The Green March', review of Anna Bramwell, *Ecology in the 20th Century: A History*, in *The Guardian* (Books section), Friday March 17, 31.

Gould, Stephen Jay (1989), *Wonderful Life: The Burgess Shale and the Nature of History*, Penguin, Harmondsworth.

Greimas, A.J. (1970), *Du Sens*, Seuil, Paris.

Grove, Richard H (1997), *Ecology, Climate and Empire: Colonialism and Global Environmental History 1400-1940*, White Horse Press, .

Habermas, Jürgen (1984), *The Theory of Communicative Action: Volume One – Reason and the Rationalisation of Society*, Polity Press, Cambridge.

Habermas, Jürgen (1987), *The Philosophical Discourse of Modernity: Twelve Lectures*, trans Frederick G. Lawrence, Polity Press, Cambridge.

Habermas, Jürgen (2003), *The Future of Human Nature*, trans William Rehg, Max Pensky and Hella Beister, Polity, Cambridge.

Hardin, Garrett (1968), 'The Tragedy of the Commons' in *Science* n. 162, 1245-8.

Hardt, Michael and Antono Negri (2000), *Empire*, Harvard University Press, Cambridge MA.

Hartley, John (1992), *The Politics of Pictures: The Creation of the Public in the Age of Popular Media*, Routledge, London.

Hegel, G.W.F. (1969), *The Science of Logic*, trans A.V. Miller, Humanities Press, New York.

Hegel, G.W.F. (1971), *Hegel's Philosophy of Mind, Being the Third Part of the Encyclopaedia of the Philosophical Sciences (1930)*, trans Willliam Wallace, Oxford University Press, Oxford.

Hegel, G.W.F. (1975), *Hegel's Logic, Being the First part of the Encyclopaedia of the Philosophical Sciences (1930)*, trans Willliam Wallace, Oxford University Press, Oxford.

Hegel, G.W.F. (1977), *The Phenomenology of Spirit* trans A.V. Miller, Oxford University Press, Oxford.

Hegel, G.W.F. (1991), *Elements of the Philosophy of Right*, trans H.B. Nisbet, Cambridge University Press, Cambridge.

Heidegger, Martin (1977), *The Question Concerning Technology and Other Essays*, trans. William Lovitt, Harper & Row, New York.

Held, David and Anthony McGrew (eds) (2000), *The Global Transformations Reader: An Introduction to the Globalization Debate*, Polity, Cambridge.

Heller, Caroline (1978), *Broadcasting and Accountability*, BFI Television Monograph 7, BFI, London.

Hobsbawm, Eric (1994), *Age of Extremes: The Short Twentieth Century 1914 - 1991*, Abacus, London.

Hochman, Jhan (1998), *Green Cultural Studies: Nature in Film, Novel and Theory*, University of Idaho Press, Moscow, Idaho.

Holden, Barry (2002), *Democracy and Global Warming*, Continuum, London.

Horkheimer, Max (1992), *Eclipse of Reason*, Continuum, New York.

House of Representatives Committee on Government Reform - Minority Staff Special Investigations Division (2003), *Politics and Science in the Bush Administration*, prepared for Rep Henry A. Waxman, August, updated November 13, http://www.reform.house.gov/min

Inglis, Fred (2000), "Edge of Darkness - Interpreting Topical Trash", in *Formations*, http://newmedia.ulst.ac.uk/phpBB/viewtopic.php?topic=2&forum=3&0

Ingram, David (2000), *Green Screen: Environmentalism and Hollywood Cinema*. University of Exeter Press, Exeter.

Jameson, Fredric (1991), *Postmodernism, or, The Cultural Logic of Late Capitalism*, Verso, London.

Jay, Martin (1993), *Downcast Eyes: The Denigration of Vision in Twentieth-Century French Thought*, University of California Press, Berkeley.

Junger, Sebastian (1997), *The Perfect Storm*, 4th Estate, London.

Kant, Immanuel (1890), *Critique of Pure Reason*, trans J.M.. Meiklejohn, George Bell and Sons, London.

Kant, Immanuel (1950), *Prolegomena to any Future Metaphysics*, ed and trans Lewis White Beck, Liberal Arts Press, New York.

Kant, Immanuel (1952), *The Critique of Judgement*, trans James Creed Meredith, Oxford University Press, Oxford.

Kant, Immanuel (1964), *Groundwork of the Metaphysics of Morals*, trans H.J. Paton, Harper Torchbooks, New York.

Kant, Immanuel (1983), 'Idea for a Universal History with a Cosmopolitan Intent' in *Perpetual Peace and Other Essays on Politics, History and Morals*, trans Ted Humphrey, Hackett Publishing, Indianapolis, 29-40.

Kelsey, Jane (1999), *Reclaiming the Future: New Zealand and the Global Economy*, Bridget Williams Books, Wellington.

Kerr, Anne and Tom Shakespeare (2002), *Genetic Politics: From Eugenics to Genome*, New Clarion Press, Cheltenham.

Kittler, Friedrich A (1999), *Gramophone, Film, Typewriter*, trans and intro Geoffrey Winthrop-Young and Michael Wutz, Stanford University Press, Stanford.

Kojève, Alexandre (1969), *Introduction to the Reading of Hegel: Lectures on the Phenomenology of Spirit,* assembled by Raymond Queneau, ed. Allan Bloom, trans James H Nichols, Jr, Cornell University Press, Ithaca.

Lash, Scott (2002), *Critique of Information*, Sage, London.

Latour, Bruno (1998), 'Drawing Things Together' in Michael Lynch and Steve Woolgar (eds), *Representation in Scientific Practice*, MIT Press, Cambridge MA., 19-68.

Lefebvre, Henri (1991), *The Production of Space*, trans Donald Nicholson-Smith, Blackwell, Oxford.

Leopold, Aldo (2001), 'Ecocentrism: The Land Ethic' in Louis P Pojman (ed), *Environmental Ethics: Readings in Theory and Application*, Wadsworth, Belmont CA., 119-126

Lévi-Strauss, Claude (1972), 'Linguistics and Anthropology' in *Structural Anthopolgy*, trans Claire Jacobson and Brooke Grundfest Schoepf, Penguin, Harmondsworth, 67-80.

Lewis, C.S. (1955), *The Abolition of Man*, Macmillan, New York.

Lippit, Akira Mizuta (2000), *Electric Animal: Toward a Rhetoric of Wildlife*, University of Minnesota Press, Minneapolis.

Lovelock, J.E., (1979), *Gaia: A New Look at Life on Earth*, Oxford University Press, Oxford.

Lotman, Yuri M (1990), *Universe of the Mind: A Semiotic Theory of Culture*, trans Ann Shukman, intro Umberto Eco, Indiana University Press, Bloomington..

Luhmann, Niklas (1986), *Love as Passion: The Codification of Intimacy*, trans Jeremy Gaines and Doris L Jones, Stanford University

Press, Stanford.

Luhmann, Niklas (1989), *Ecological Communication*, trans John Bednarz Jr., University of Chicago Press, Chicago.

Luhmann, Niklas (2000), *The Reality of the Mass Media*, trans Kathleen Cross, Stanford University Press, Stanford.

Lukács, Georg (1969), *The Historical Novel*, trans Hannah and Stanley Mitchell, Peregrine, Harmondsworth.

Lukács, Georg (1971), 'Reification and the Consciousness of the Proletariat' in *History and Class Consciousness: Studies in Marxist Dialectic*, trans Rodney Livingstone, MIT Press, Cambridge, MA, 83-222.

Lyotard, Jean François (1978), 'Acinema', trans J-F Lyotard and Paisley N Livingstone, *Wide Angle* vol 2 n 3, 52-9; reprinted in Lyotard, Jean François (1989), *The Lyotard Reader*, ed Andrew Benjamin, Blackwell, Oxford, 169-80.

Lyotard, Jean-François (1984), *The Postmodern Condition: A Report on Knowledge*, trans Geoff Bennington and Brian Massumi, Manchester University Press, Manchester.

Lyotard, Jean François (1994), *Lessons on the Analytic of the Sublime*, trans Elizabeth Rottenberg, Stanford University Press, Stanford.

Malone, JJ (1966), *Pine Trees and Politics: The Naval Stores and Forest Policy in Colonial New England, 1691-1775*, Oxford University Press, Oxford.

Marks, Laura U (2000), *The Skin of the Film: Intercultural Cinema, Embodiment, and the Senses*, Duke University Press, Durham NC.

Marx, Karl (1975), 'The Economic and Philosophical Manuscripts' in *Early Writings*, trans Rodney Livingstone and Gregor Benton, NLB/ Viking, New York, 279-400.

Marx, Leo (1964), *The Machine in the Garden: Technology and the Pastoral Ideal in America*, Oxford University Press, New York.

Merleau-Ponty, Maurice (1962), *The Phenomenology of Perception*, trans Colin Smith, Routledge Classics, London.

McArthur, Colin (1978), *Television and History*, BFI Television Monograph 8, BFI, London.

McCarthy, Anna (2001), *Ambient Television: Visual Culture and Public Space*, Duke University Press, Durham NC.

McLuhan, Marshall and Bruce R Powers (1989), *The Global Village: Transformations in World Life and Media in the 21st Century*, Oxford University Press, Oxford.

Miller, Toby, Nitin Govil, John McMurria and Richard Maxwell (2001), *Global Hollywood*, BFI, London.

Mumford, Lewis (1934), *Technics and Civilization*, Routledge and Kegan Paul, London.

Nancy, Jean-Luc (1993), *The Experience of Freedom*, trans Bridget McDonald, foreword Peter Fenves, Stanford University Press, Stanford.

Napier, Susan J (2001), *Anime From Akira to Princess Mononoke: Experiencing Contemporary Japanese Animation*, Palgrave, New York.

Neale, Steve (1980), *Genre*, BFI, London.

New Zealand Institute of Economic Research (2002), *Scoping the Lasting Effects of* The Lord of the Rings*: Report to the New Zealand Film Commission*, NZIER, Wellington, April.

Orwell, George (1951), *Animal Farm*, Penguin, Harmondsworth.

Parisi, Paula (1998), *Titanic and the Making of James Cameron*, Orion, London.

Peirce, Charles Sanders (1991), *Peirce on Signs: Writings on Semiotic by Charles Sanders Peirce*, ed James Hooper, University of North Carolina Press, Chapel Hill.

Plumwood, Val (2002), *Environmental Culture: The Ecologoical Crisis of Reason*, Routledge, London.

Portmann, Adolf (1967), *Animal Forms and Patterns: A Study of the Appearance of Animals*, trans Hella Czech, Shocken, New York.

Pound, Ezra (1964), *The Cantos of Ezra Pound*, Faber, London.

Raustiala, Kal (2001), 'Nonstate Actors in the Global Climate Regime' in Urs Luterbacher and Detlef F. Sprinz (eds), *International Relations and Global Climate Change*, MIT Press, Cambridge MA.

Ridley, Matt (1999), *Genome: The Autobiography of a Species in 23 Chapters*, 4th Estate, London.

Rolston III, Holmes (2001), 'Naturalizing Values: Organisms and Species' in Louis P Pojman (ed), *Environmental Ethics: Readings in Theory and Application*, Wadsworth, Belmont CA., 76-86

Rose, Jacqueline (1984), *The Case of Peter Pan or The Impossibility of Children's Fiction*, Macmillan, London.

Rosenau, James N (1990), *Turbulence in World Politic: A Theory of Change and Continuity*, Princeton University Press, Princeton.

Rosenau, James N (2003), *Distant Proximities: Dynamics Beyond*

Globalization, Princeton University Press, Princeton.

Scannell, Paddy (1996), *Radio, Television, and Modern Life : A Phenomenological Approach*, Blackwell, Oxford.

Schama, Simon (1995), *Landscape and Memory*, Harper Collins, London.

Schatz, Thomas (1981), *Hollywood Genres: Formulas, Filmmaking and the Studio System*, Random House, New York.

Sebeok, Thomas A (1991), '"Animal" in Biological and Semiotic Perpective' in Iris Smith (ed), *American Signatures: Semiotic Inquiry and Method*, University of Oklahoma Press, Norman, 159-173.

Silverman, Kaja (2000), *World Spectators*, Stanford University Press, Stanford.

Slide, Anthony (ed) (1982), *Selected Film Criticism 1896-1911*, The Scarecrow Press, Metuchen NJ.

Smythe, Dallas (1994), 'Communications: Blindspot of Western Marxism [1977]' in Smythe, , *Counterclockwise: Perspectives on Communication*, ed Thomas Guback, Westview Press, Boulder CO., 266-291; reprinted from *Canadian Journal of Political and Social Theory*, v.1 n.3, Fall 1977, pp 1-27. .

Spigel, Lynn (1992), *Make Room for TV: Television and the Family Ideal in Postwar America*, University of Chicago Press, Chicago.

Stafford, Barbara (1994), *Artful Science: Enlightenment Entertainment and the Eclipse of Visual Education*, MIT Press, Cambridge MA.

Stiglitz, Joseph (2002), *Globalization and its Discontents*, Penguin, London.

Thacker, Eugene (2004), *Biomedia*, University of Minnesota Press, Minneapolis.

Tolkien, J.R.R. (2001 [1954-5]), *The Lord of the Rings*, Harper Collins, New York..

UNESCO (1997), *Universal Declaration on the Human Genome and Human Rights*, http://www.unesco.org/shs/human_rights/hrbc.htm, accessed 12 May 2004.

United Nations (1948), *Universal Declaration of Human Rights*, http://www.un.org/Overview/rights.html, accessed 12 May 2004.

Virilio, Paul (1996), *Un paysage d'événements*, Galilée, Paris; (2000), *A Landscape of Events*, trans Julie Rose, MIT PressCambridge MA..

Virilio, Paul (1998), *Cybermonde: la politique du pire*, entretien avec Phillippe Petit, textuel/Seuil, Paris.; *The Politics of the Very Worst*, trans Sylvère Lottringer and Michael Cavaliere, Semiotext(e), New York.

Virilio, Paul and Sylvère Lottringer (2002), *Crepuscular Dawn*, trans Mike Taormina, Semiotext(e), New York.

Watkins, Peter (2001), 'La Commune de Paris', http://www.peterwatkins.it, accessed 1 August 2003.

Weber, Samuel (1985), 'Afterword' in Lyotard, Jean-François and Jean-Loup Thébaud (1985), *Just Gaming*, trans Wlad Godzich, University of Minnesota Press, Minneapolis.

Weber, Samuel (1996), *Mass Mediauras: Form Technics Media*, ed Alan Cholodenko, Power Publications, Sydney.

White, Mimi (1986), 'Crossing Wavelengths: The Diegetic and Referential Imaginary of American Commercial Television' in *Cinema Journal* v.25 n.2, Winter, 51-64.

Williams, Raymond (1974), *Television: Technology and Cultural Form*, Fontana, London.

Williams, Raymond (1983), *Towards 2000*, London, Chatto and Windus.

Wilson, Alexander (1991), *The Culture of Nature: North American Landscape from Disney to the Exxon Valdez*, Between the Lines, Toronto.

Wilson, Edward O (2002), *The Future of Life*, Abacus, London.

Wittgenstein, Ludwig (1968), *Philosophical Investigations*, 2nd edn., trans G.E.M. Anscombe, Basil Blackwell, Oxford.

Wolfe, Cary (2003), 'In the Shadow of Wttgenstein's Lion: Language, Ethics, and the Question of the Animal' in Wolfe, Cary (ed) (2003), *Zoontologies: The Question of the Animal*, University of Minnesota Press, Minneapolis, 1-57.

Filmography

The Abyss (Special Edition), James Cameron, 1989,Twentieth Century Fox, 164 mins, US

Antz, Eric Darnell, Tim Johnson, 1998, DreamWorks, 83 ins, US

The Ascent of Man, scr/presenter Jakob Bronowski, May 5 - July 28 1973, BBC, 13 parts, UK

Atlantis, Luc Besson, 1992, Gaumont / Cecchi Gori / Tiger, 75 mins, France / Italy

Babe, Chris Noonan, 1995, Kennedy Miller Productions / Universal Pictures, 94 mins, Australia

Bambi, David Hand, 1942, Disney, 70 mins, US.

Blade Runner, Ridley Scott, The Ladd Company, 1982, 112 mins, US

Blue Planet: A Natural History of the Oceans, Series producer Alastair Fothergill; Producers Martha Holmes and Andy Byatt, 2002, BBC / Discovery Channel, 535 mins (8 x 55 mins): 1. The Blue Planet; 2. The Deep; 3. Open Ocean; 4. Frozen Seas; 5. Seasonal Seas; 6. Coral Seas; 7. Tidal Seas; 8. Coasts; + 'Making Waves' and 'Deep Trouble' (BBC/WWW), UK

A Bug's Life, John Lasseter, Disney / Pixar, 96 mins, US.

Captain Video, Spencer Gordon Bennett, Wallace A Grissell, 1951, DuMont, 15 chapters, US

Chicken Run, Peter Lord and Nick Park, Dreamworks / Pathé / Aardman, 2001, 84 mins

City of Lost Children, Jean-Pierre Jeunet and Marc Caro, Entertainment/Lumiere Pictures/Canal Plus/France 3 Cinema, France, 1995, 112 mins

Civilisation, p. Michael Gill, Peter Montagnon, scr/presented Kenneth Clark, 23 February - 18 May 1969, BBC, 13 episodes, UK.

Close Encounters of the Third Kind: Special Edition, Steven Spielberg, 1977/1980, Columbia/EMI, USA,

Cold Mountain, Anthony Minghella, 2004, Miramax Films / Mirage Enterprises / Bona Fide Productions, 152 min, US

C.S.I., Creators Anthony Zuiker , Josh Berman, 2000- , Alliance Atlantis Communications / Arc Entertainment / CBS / Jerry Bruckheimer Television / Alliance Atlantis

Daredevil, Mark Steven Johnson, 2003, 20th Century Fox / Horseshoe Bay Productions / Marvel Enterprises / New Regency Pictures / Regency Enterprises, 103 mins, US

The Day After Tomorrow, Roland Emmerich, 2004, Tomorrow Films / 20th Century Fox / Centropolis Entertainment / Lions Gate Entertainment / Mark Gordon Productions. 124 mins, US

Death on the Rock, reporter Julian Manyon, presenter Jonathan Dimbleby, 28 April 1988, Thames Television / ITV, UK

Delicatessen, Jean-Pierre Jeunet, Marc Caro, 1990, Sofinergie Films / La Sofica Sofinergie 2 / Investimage 2 / Sofica Investimage 3 / Fondation GAN pour le Cinéma / Constellation / Hachette Première / Union Générale Cinématographique / Victoires Productions [fr]99 mins, France

Le Dernier Combat, Luc Besson, 1983, Gaumont/Les Films du Loup, 89 mins

Edge of Darkness, scr: Troy Kennedy-Martin; dir: Martin Campbell; Producer: Michael Wearing, BBC2, 6 x 55 Minutes: 04/11/85 1: Compassionate Leave; 11/11/85 2: Into the Shadows; 18/11/85 3: Burden of Proof; 25/11/85 4: Breakthrough; 02/12/85 5: Northmoor; 09/12/85 6: Fusion

The Fast and the Furious, Rob Cohen, 2001, Mediastream Film / Neal H. Moritz Productions / Original Film / Universal Pictures, 107 mins, Gemany / US

The Fifth Element, Luc Besson,1998, Columbia Pictures / Gaumont, 123 mins

Finding Nemo, Andrew Stanton, 2003, Walt Disney Pictures / Pixar Pictures, 97 mins

First Spaceship on Venus (*Der Schweigende Stern*), Kurt Maetzig, 1960, DEFA/Illuzjon Film Unit, 94 mins, East Germany/Poland

Forbidden Planet, Fred McLeod Wilcox, MGM, 1956, 99 mins US

Free Willy, Simon Wincer, 1993, Alcor Films / Le Studio Canal+ / Regency Enterprises / Warner Bros, 112 mins, US.

Gettysburg, Ronald F Maxwell, 1993, Esparza/Katz Productions / Turner Pictures, Part 1 136 mins; Part 2 118 mins, US

Glory, Edward Zwick, 1989, TriStar Pictures, 133 mins, US.

Godzilla, Roland Emmerich, 1998, Centropolis Entertainment / Fried Films / Independent Pictures/ TriStar, 133 mins, US

GoldenEye, Martin Campbell, 1995, MGM-UA/Albert R Broccoli, 124 mins, UK / US

The Grapes of Wrath, John Ford, 1940, Twentieth Century Fox, 129 mins, US

The Great Escape, John Sturges, 1962, The Mirisch Corporation / UA, 173 mins, US / West Germany

High Treason, Maurice Elvey, 1929, Gaumont British, 95 mins, UK

Hulk, Ang Lee, 2003, Universal / Marvel Enterprises / Valhalla / Good Machine Productions, 137 mins, US

International House, Edward Sutherland, 1933, Paramount, 70 mins, US

King Lear, Grigori Kosintsev, 1970, Lenfilm Studio, 139 mins, USSR

The Last Combat (*Le Dernier Combat*), Luc Besson, 1983, Gaumont/ Les Films du Loup, 89 mins

The Last of the Mohicans, Michael Mann, 1992, Morgan Creek Intl, 108 mins

Life On Earth, presenter David Attenborough, 1979, BBC, 12 episodes, UK

Lord Jim, Richard Brooks, 1964, Columbia Pictures Corporation / Keep Films, 154 mins, UK

The Lord of the Rings: The Fellowship of the Ring, Peter Jackson, New Line / Wingnut, 2002, 225 mins, (extended edn), US / NZ.

The Lord of the Rings: The Two Towers, Peter Jackson, New Line / Wingnut, 2003, 225 mins, (extended edn), US / NZ

The Lord of the Rings: The Return of the King, Peter Jackson, New Line / Wingnut, 2003, 210 mins, US / NZ

Man of Arran, Robert Flaherty, 1934, Gainsborough Pictures / Gaumont British / The Rank Organisation, 75 mins, UK

The Mask of Zorro, Martin Campbell, 1998, Amblin Entertainment / TriStar Pictures / Zorro Productions138 mins, US

The Matrix, The Wachowski Brothers, 1999, Village Roadshow / Grouch II Film Partnership/ Warner Bros/ Silver Pictures, 130 mins, US

The Matrix Reloaded, The Wachowski Brothers, 2003, Village Roadshow/Warner Bros / NPV Entertainment / Silver Pictures, 132 mins, US

Matrix Revolutions, The Wachowski Brothers, 2003, Village Roadshow, Warner Bros / NPV Entertainment / Silver Pictures, 124 mins, US

Our Friends in the North, Directors Simon Cellan Jones, Pedr James, Stuart Urban, Writers Peter Flannery, Charles Pattinson, executive producer Michael Wearing, 1996, BBC, 9 x 70 min episodes, UK.

The Patriot, Roland Emmerich, 2000, Columbia / Mutual / Centropolis, 165 mins, US

The Perfect Storm, Wolfgang Peterson, 2000, Warner Bros/ Baltimore Spring Creek/ Radiant Productions, 125 mins, US

The Phantom Empire, Otto Brower, B. Reeves Eason, 1936, Mascott, 12 chapters, US.

Planet of the Apes, Franklin J Schaffner, 1967, Twenith Century Fox, US, 107 mins, US

Princess Mononoke, Hayao Miyazaki, Tokuma Shoten/ Nippon Television Network/ Dentsu / Studio Ghibli/ Miramax, 128 mins, Japan

Rescued By Rover, Lewis Fitzhamn, 1905, Cecil Hepworth, 7 mins, UK

Signs, M Night Shyamalan, 2002, Blinding Edge Pictures / The Kennedy/Marshall Company / Touchstone Pictures, 106 mins, US

The Sixth Sense, M Night Shyamalan, 1999, Hollywood Pictures / Spyglass Entertainment / The Kennedy/Marshall Company, 107 mins, US

Soylent Green, Richard Fleischer, 1973, MGM, 97 mins, US

Spiderman, Sam Raimi, 2002, Columbia Pictures Corporation / Marvel Enterprises / Laura Ziskin Productions, 121 mins, US

*State of Play*Director David Yates, Writer Paul Abbott , Producer Hilary Bevan Jones, 2003, BBC / Endor Productions

Subway, Luc Besson, 1985, Gaumont International, Les Films du Loup, TF1 Films Productions, TSF Productions, 94 mins, France

Themroc, Claude Faraldo, 1972, Filmanthrope / Les Productions FDL, 110 mins, France

Titanic, James Cameron, 1997, 20th Century Fox/Paramount/ Lightstorm, 195 mins, US

12 Monkeys, Terry Gilliam, 1995, Universal / Atlas Entertainment, 124 mins, US

24, Joel Surnow, Robert Cochran (creators), 2001-, Imagine Entertainment / 20th Century Fox / Imagine Television / Real Time Productions, 3 x 24 episodes,

Vertical Limit, Martin Campbell, 2000, Columbia / Global Entertainment Productions GmbH, Mountain High Productions, 124 mins, US / Germany

Whale Rider, Niki Caro,2003, South Pacific Pictures / Apollomedia/ Pandora Film/ NZ Film Production Fund / NZ Film Commission / New Zealand On Air, 97 mins

The X Files, Chris Carter (creator),1993 - 2002, 20th Century Fox Television, Ten Thirteen Productions

X-Men, Bryan Singer, 2000, 20th Century Fox/Marvel Entertainment/ The Donners' Company/Bad Hat Harry, 100 mins, US / Canada

X-Men 2, Bryan Singer, 2003, 20th Century Fox/Marvel Entertainment/The Donners' Company/Bad Hat Harry, 128 mins, US / Canada

Index